The SaaS Architecture

Scalable, Secure, and Performance

The SaaS Architecture

Scalable, Secure, and Performance

Vinu V Das

Tabor Press

ISBN: 978-1-997541-04-2

Table of Contents

Chapter 1: Introduction to SaaS Architecture

1.1 Understanding SaaS

The concept of **Software as a Service (SaaS)** has revolutionized how businesses, organizations, and individual users consume and deploy software. Instead of following a traditional approach in which software is purchased or licensed and then installed on local machines or organizational servers, SaaS enables users to access applications via the internet on a subscription or pay-as-you-go basis. This shift has been driven by numerous factors, including the desire for reduced upfront costs, improved accessibility, and the need to handle evolving technology more flexibly.

Over the last two decades, internet connectivity and cloud computing have matured to a point where SaaS offerings have become not just a viable option but a dominant model in many software markets. The hallmark of SaaS lies in how it abstracts away hardware provisioning, software maintenance, and version updates—allowing customers to focus on using the software rather than managing its underlying infrastructure. To fully understand why SaaS has become so prevalent, one must first look at its key characteristics, its distinction from other software delivery models, and how its evolution reflects broader shifts in the technology landscape.

By exploring both the technical and business perspectives, readers will appreciate why SaaS architecture requires a distinct mindset compared to older software models. This chapter introduces fundamental terminologies, sets the stage for deeper discussions in subsequent chapters, and provides a concise overview of the challenges and benefits SaaS brings to the modern software ecosystem.

1.1.1 Definition and Key Characteristics

Definition of SaaS

Software as a Service is most often described as a software distribution model in which a cloud provider hosts applications and makes them available to end users over the internet. The software and its associated data are typically hosted in one or more data centers, leveraging either public, private, or hybrid cloud infrastructure. Customers, whether individuals or organizations, pay for the software on a subscription basis—commonly monthly or yearly—or sometimes on a usage basis determined by factors such as the number of transactions or the volume of data processed.

Unlike traditional licensed software, where the buyer must manage every aspect of running the application (including hardware procurement, software installation, patches, and upgrades), the SaaS provider assumes these responsibilities. This fundamental shift changes the economics of software, turning large capital expenditures into more predictable operational expenses. It also relieves organizations from the burden of employing specialized personnel for patching, version control, and infrastructure management—thus allowing them to direct more resources to strategic initiatives.

Key Characteristics

Several foundational features set SaaS apart from other software delivery mechanisms:

1. **Hosted in the Cloud**: SaaS applications are deployed on servers in the cloud, which means that end users do not need to install software locally. Organizations can scale up or down based on usage demands without significant hardware or software investments. This cloud-based foundation enables robust reliability through distributed infrastructure, automatic failover, and global availability zones—although the specific reliability mechanisms vary depending on the provider's architecture.

2. **On-Demand Access**: End users can access SaaS applications anytime, from nearly any internet-connected device. This universal accessibility makes SaaS particularly attractive in an era where remote work, mobile computing, and global collaboration are common. As long as users can connect to the service over HTTP or HTTPS, they can log in securely to perform their tasks.

3. **Subscription or Pay-Per-Use Pricing**: Most SaaS providers charge periodic subscription fees, which can be based on various factors such as the number of seats (i.e., number of user accounts), the volume of data processed, or the specific features accessed. Some may also offer pay-per-use pricing or tiered service levels that allow users to choose a plan that best suits their needs and budget.

4. **Multi-Tenancy**: A critical component of many SaaS solutions is the idea that a single codebase and infrastructure can serve multiple customers—referred to as tenants—while logically isolating and protecting their data. Through clever database

schemas or containerization approaches, providers can ensure that each tenant's data remains separate while offering economies of scale. This is a defining architectural principle that enables providers to manage upgrades, patches, and resource allocation efficiently.

5. **Automated Upgrades and Maintenance**: In a SaaS environment, the provider takes responsibility for regularly updating the platform, fixing bugs, adding new features, and ensuring overall availability. These updates often happen transparently, with minimal user disruption. Customers benefit from always having access to the latest version of the software without needing to plan major IT projects for each new release.

6. **Rapid Deployment and Integration**: Deploying or provisioning new user accounts within a SaaS environment can be as simple as creating a new subscription plan or adding seats under an existing plan. Integration with other SaaS or on-premises systems can also be streamlined through APIs provided by the vendor, along with standardized protocols like REST, SOAP, or GraphQL. Although this can become more complex in larger enterprises, the general principle is that SaaS solutions reduce the overhead associated with rolling out a new system.

Overall, these key characteristics illustrate how SaaS differs sharply from older models. Together, they create an environment that fosters agility, scalability, and operational efficiency for both customers and providers.

Strategic Implications of These Characteristics

From a strategic standpoint, the characteristics of SaaS also influence how businesses and software providers position themselves. Traditional vendors have had to adjust their licensing structures to remain competitive with SaaS newcomers; at the same time, enterprises looking to adopt SaaS must rethink their procurement, budgeting, and IT governance processes. These shifts require a high-level strategic perspective that touches finance, HR, compliance, and even corporate culture. Consequently, understanding SaaS is not just about technology—it is also about business transformation.

1.1.2 Evolution of Software Delivery Models

To fully appreciate the significance of SaaS in the modern era, one must look at how we arrived at this point. Over the last few decades, the software industry has witnessed multiple paradigm shifts in how software is developed, distributed, and consumed. A brief historical overview reveals how the drive for simplicity, scalability, and global reach has influenced the widespread adoption of SaaS.

On-Premises Software

The earliest widespread model for delivering software involved physical media (such as floppy disks and CDs) provided to customers, who would then install the software on their own servers or personal computers. Maintenance, upgrades, and troubleshooting fell squarely on the shoulders of the customers, with occasional support from the software vendor. This model demanded substantial upfront hardware and licensing costs, as well as dedicated teams to manage updates and ensure system stability. Despite these drawbacks, on-premises software dominated during the early days of enterprise computing, partly because robust internet connectivity was not universally available to support remote hosting at scale.

Application Service Providers (ASPs)

In the late 1990s and early 2000s, as the internet matured, **Application Service Providers** emerged. ASPs hosted software on behalf of multiple clients, usually customizing each instance for a specific customer. While ASPs eased some of the burden on organizations by handling certain aspects of maintenance and hosting, the heavy customization often made them costly and inefficient. This approach lacked the streamlined multi-tenancy and self-service provisioning that are hallmarks of modern SaaS. Nonetheless, ASPs represented an important stepping stone, as they demonstrated the feasibility of remotely hosted software.

Rise of Cloud Computing

With the rise of **cloud computing**—driven by major technology vendors offering virtualized servers, storage, and networking—applications no longer needed to be limited by local hardware constraints. Cloud infrastructure providers like Amazon Web Services (AWS), Microsoft Azure, and Google Cloud Platform offered on-demand compute resources, pay-as-you-go pricing, and automated scalability. This evolution drastically reduced the barrier to entry for software companies that wished to build hosted applications accessible through the internet.

Emergence of SaaS

Capitalizing on these cloud computing models, SaaS emerged as a more standardized and repeatable form of delivering software. Instead of customizing installations for each client, SaaS vendors often adopt a single codebase that can serve many tenants. The benefits of continuous updates, centralized hosting, and subscription-based billing resonated with both small businesses and large enterprises. Salesforce, launched in 1999, is often cited as a pioneer in popularizing the SaaS model, particularly for Customer Relationship Management (CRM). Over time, hundreds of other successful SaaS solutions appeared in areas ranging from human resources and accounting to marketing automation and data analytics.

Contemporary Landscape

In the contemporary technology landscape, SaaS is no longer a niche offering but a mainstream distribution model. Virtually every major software category has seen the emergence of multiple SaaS providers. The pandemic-era push for remote collaboration further intensified reliance on SaaS solutions, since they provide reliable, location-agnostic access. Additionally, startups have found SaaS a particularly attractive delivery model due to its predictable revenue streams and close alignment with agile product development processes.

SaaS vs. Other Cloud Models

Within the broader scope of cloud computing, SaaS is often mentioned alongside **Infrastructure as a Service (IaaS)** and **Platform as a Service (PaaS)**:

- **IaaS** focuses on providing basic building blocks of computing resources—virtual machines, storage volumes, and networking—on a pay-as-you-go basis.
- **PaaS** takes things a step further by offering developers a managed environment to build, test, and deploy applications.
- **SaaS**, by contrast, is the final layer where fully developed applications are delivered to end users over the internet.

While IaaS and PaaS target software developers and IT professionals, SaaS caters to a broad audience, often including non-technical end users, managers, and executives. The popularity of SaaS stems from its ability to shield these users from infrastructure-level decisions and complexities.

Why SaaS Matters Today

SaaS holds particular significance in a business environment that requires rapid innovation, continuous delivery, and minimal overhead. As technology refresh cycles shorten, enterprises no longer wish to be saddled with aging infrastructure or outdated software. Moreover, the subscription model aligns with a shift toward operational expenditures (OpEx) rather than capital expenditures (CapEx). This alignment can boost profitability, agility, and competitiveness across industries.

Overall, the evolution from on-premises software to SaaS illustrates a broader trend: technology is becoming more abstracted, more accessible, and more integrated into everyday workflows, transcending geographic and organizational boundaries.

1.2 Benefits of SaaS

Having established the fundamentals of SaaS and traced its evolution through earlier software delivery models, it is essential to understand the core benefits that have fueled its widespread adoption. While other software models each have their advantages, SaaS is particularly well-suited to an era defined by rapid change, global collaboration, and continuous demands for innovation.

1.2.1 Cost-Effectiveness and Scalability

Cost-Effectiveness

 One of the most commonly cited advantages of SaaS is its cost-effectiveness. Traditionally, organizations investing in software faced significant upfront costs, including hardware acquisition, data center construction or leasing, software licenses, and the labor needed to install, configure, and test these systems. Additionally, ongoing maintenance expenses—such as system patches, security updates, and version upgrades—added another layer of financial and operational burden.

With SaaS, most of these costs shift onto the provider:

1. **Reduced Capital Expenditure**: Instead of purchasing physical servers and data center capacity, organizations utilize the SaaS provider's infrastructure. This eliminates large capital outlays and corresponding depreciation schedules, replacing them with regular subscription fees or pay-per-use costs that

can be categorized as operational expenses. By converting CapEx to OpEx, companies gain financial flexibility, preserving cash for more strategic investments.

2. **Lower Support Overhead**: Because the provider handles application maintenance, bug fixes, and updates, internal IT teams can focus on higher-level tasks. This may yield further cost savings by reducing the need for highly specialized staff to manage each piece of software internally.

3. **Predictable Budgeting**: SaaS subscriptions typically come with transparent pricing structures, which may be tiered based on feature sets, number of users, or usage volume. This allows organizations to plan their budgets more accurately and avoid the unwelcome surprises that can occur with on-premises systems (e.g., hardware failures necessitating expensive replacements).

4. **Economies of Scale**: Because multiple customers share the underlying infrastructure in a multi-tenant environment, providers can distribute costs more efficiently, often passing some of these savings to customers. This is especially valuable for smaller businesses that would otherwise struggle to afford enterprise-grade capabilities.

Scalability

In addition to cost advantages, SaaS solutions are inherently scalable. Whether an organization experiences rapid growth or faces seasonal fluctuations in demand, SaaS providers can automatically adjust resources to accommodate these changes. This auto-scaling capability is typically built on top of cloud platforms that offer near-limitless compute and storage capacity.

1. **Rapid Upscaling**: If a business gains new users or sees an increase in data processing requirements, the SaaS provider

can add more server capacity, memory, or bandwidth behind the scenes. End users often experience this as a seamless transition, with little or no downtime.

2. **Eliminating Over-Provisioning**: Conversely, if an organization has a temporary drop in usage—for example, a seasonal decline—SaaS billing can scale down, reducing costs. In a traditional model, the organization would likely have over-purchased hardware or licenses to accommodate peak loads, resulting in wasted capacity during off-peak times.

3. **Immediate Global Reach**: Larger SaaS providers often run data centers in multiple geographic regions, enabling companies to support global user bases. This distributed infrastructure can minimize latency and ensure business continuity if one location becomes inaccessible.

Strategic Business Value

The combined benefits of cost-effectiveness and scalability do not merely impact IT budgets—they also influence the strategic direction and competitive positioning of a company. SaaS solutions enable faster product development cycles and quicker time to market, as well as fostering an experimental mindset where new features can be tested with subsets of users before a general release. By lowering financial and operational barriers to accessing state-of-the-art software, SaaS helps level the playing field across companies of various sizes and across different industries.

1.2.2 Accessibility and Multi-Tenancy

Accessibility

Another key advantage of SaaS is its high accessibility for diverse user groups. Users can typically log in to a SaaS application through a standard web browser or dedicated mobile apps, reducing the need for specialized software or hardware. This accessibility opens the door for new ways of working:

1. **Remote and Distributed Teams**: In modern workplaces, team members may be geographically dispersed, working from different continents or time zones. SaaS is uniquely suited to supporting remote and distributed teams, as all they need is a reliable internet connection and login credentials. This is pivotal for organizations embracing hybrid or fully remote work arrangements.

2. **Multiple Device Support**: SaaS applications often support desktops, laptops, tablets, and smartphones across various operating systems. By offering a consistent interface and ensuring data synchronization across devices, SaaS helps businesses foster productivity, regardless of the platform employees or customers use.

3. **Rapid Onboarding**: Because there is minimal need for local installation or configuration, onboarding new users is often reduced to creating an account and assigning a role or license type. This quick process not only saves time but also enhances user satisfaction right from the start.

Multi-Tenancy

One of the core architectural concepts underpinning SaaS is **multi-tenancy**. This means that a single instance (or codebase) of the software runs on a shared infrastructure while serving multiple customer organizations (tenants). Each tenant's data remains isolated, but logically, they share resources such as compute power and storage.

1. **Efficient Resource Utilization**: By pooling resources like CPU, memory, and storage, SaaS providers can distribute usage peaks and valleys among multiple tenants. This improves overall efficiency and can reduce operational costs,

part of which can be passed on to customers through more competitive pricing.

2. **Simplified Upgrades and Maintenance**: Rather than managing dozens or hundreds of separate software instances—each with its own version and patch level—SaaS vendors can update the codebase once. All tenants benefit from new features or bug fixes simultaneously, improving the overall customer experience. This uniformity also makes support easier, as all customers use the same version of the software.

3. **Enhanced Collaboration**: With multiple organizations effectively sharing a platform, integration and data exchange between different entities can become more seamless. This is particularly advantageous in supply chain scenarios where multiple partners or vendors need to exchange information rapidly.

4. **Security Considerations**: While multi-tenancy can initially raise concerns about data separation and security, modern SaaS architectures employ robust logical and physical mechanisms to protect sensitive information. A well-designed multi-tenant platform can offer security standards that rival or exceed what many organizations could implement on-premises. Security is often further enhanced by large-scale investments in data encryption, intrusion detection, and vulnerability management that would be cost-prohibitive for smaller or medium-sized enterprises to replicate on their own.

Balancing Accessibility and Complexity

Despite its accessibility and shared-resource model, a SaaS environment can become complex if it attempts to cater to many distinct use cases under one umbrella. Providers must navigate the trade-offs between standardization (which keeps maintenance costs down and simplifies user support) and customization (which allows specific industry or organizational needs to be addressed). Managing these trade-offs is crucial for SaaS providers seeking to remain flexible without introducing unsustainable complexity.

1.3 Challenges in SaaS Development

While SaaS architecture brings many advantages, it is by no means a silver bullet. Providers and consumers of SaaS solutions both face challenges that can affect adoption, deployment, user satisfaction, and long-term sustainability. This section sheds light on some of the main issues that arise in SaaS environments and outlines why addressing them effectively is crucial from the earliest stages of planning and design.

1.3.1 Security and Compliance Concerns

Security in a Shared Environment

One of the foremost challenges in SaaS development is ensuring robust security. By design, SaaS applications operate in a multi-tenant environment where multiple customers' data resides on the same infrastructure. While sophisticated logical partitions and cryptographic measures help isolate each tenant's data, perceived or real vulnerabilities in this setup can deter organizations that handle sensitive information, such as financial institutions or healthcare providers.

Key security considerations include:

1. **Data Isolation**: Ensuring that no tenant can inadvertently or maliciously access another tenant's data is paramount. Design flaws in database schemas, access controls, or APIs can lead to breaches that erode trust and incur legal liabilities.

2. **Endpoint Security**: Because SaaS applications are accessible over the internet, they are inherently exposed to a wide range

of cyber threats, including Distributed Denial of Service (DDoS) attacks, brute force login attempts, phishing, or zero-day exploits. Providers need to implement robust perimeter defenses, intrusion detection systems, and network monitoring to protect the service.

3. **Secure APIs**: Many SaaS solutions rely on APIs for integration with other systems. These integration points must be carefully secured to prevent unauthorized access, injection attacks, or data leaks. Proper authentication, rate limiting, and request validation are all essential in mitigating these risks.

4. **Insider Threats**: Even with external threats addressed, insider threats—either from employees of the SaaS provider or employees of a tenant—can pose significant risks. Comprehensive logging, strict role-based access controls, and real-time auditing can help mitigate these vulnerabilities.

Compliance Landscape

Organizations may need to adhere to an array of **compliance standards** and regulations depending on the industry and the geographical regions where they operate. Examples include:

- **General Data Protection Regulation (GDPR)** in the European Union, focusing on data protection and privacy.
- **Health Insurance Portability and Accountability Act (HIPAA)** in the United States, which sets standards for protecting sensitive patient data in healthcare.
- **Payment Card Industry Data Security Standard (PCI DSS)** for companies that handle credit card information.
- **Sarbanes-Oxley Act (SOX)** in the United States, concerning corporate financial reporting.

For a SaaS provider, achieving compliance means implementing security measures, organizational policies, and governance frameworks that satisfy one or multiple regulatory bodies. This can be complex, especially if the software is offered globally, where laws and regulations vary. From a design perspective, compliance affects everything from how data is stored and encrypted to how user consent is obtained and documented.

Trust and Reputation

Security and compliance play an outsized role in establishing trust between SaaS providers and their customers. Even one high-profile data breach can damage a provider's reputation irreparably. Conversely, demonstrating a rigorous approach to security and passing independent audits (e.g., SOC 2) can attract enterprises that must meet strict internal governance standards.

1.3.2 Performance and Availability

Performance Expectations in SaaS

In a SaaS context, performance is more than just application speed—it is also about consistency, responsiveness, and the ability to handle sudden spikes in traffic or usage. Customers expect the application to be available around the clock with minimal latency. If the SaaS solution is business-critical (e.g., a CRM system managing sales leads), any downtime or significant slowdowns can translate into lost revenue and frayed customer relationships.

Key performance considerations include:

1. **Latency and Response Times**: SaaS applications may be accessed by users in different geographic regions. Ensuring low latency often involves employing globally distributed content delivery networks (CDNs), edge computing nodes, or multi-region failover strategies. While this may not require as much detail as future chapters will cover, at an introductory

level, it is important to note that the architecture must be designed with geographic diversity in mind.

2. **Scalability**: Although scalability is typically a benefit of SaaS, poorly designed architectures can lead to bottlenecks. For instance, if the application relies on a single relational database that cannot efficiently handle the read/write load of thousands of concurrent users, performance will degrade. Strategies for caching, sharding, or employing NoSQL databases can come into play, but these must be carefully planned from the start.

3. **Resource Quotas and Limits**: Cloud infrastructure providers often impose quotas on compute, storage, or networking resources. SaaS developers must track these quotas to ensure that usage spikes do not trigger performance throttling or force the application to stop serving requests. Implementing autoscaling rules and load balancing across multiple instances can help mitigate these risks.

4. **Code Efficiency**: Performance also depends on how efficiently the application handles requests. Inefficient code, memory leaks, or resource-intensive tasks can slow down the entire service. As the user base grows, these inefficiencies become more pronounced, requiring proactive monitoring and optimization.

Availability and Uptime

In the SaaS model, availability is often formalized through **Service Level Agreements (SLAs)** that promise certain uptime percentages (e.g., 99.9% or 99.99%). Achieving these levels of uptime requires robust strategies for:

1. **Redundancy**: Critical components of the infrastructure must be duplicated or multiplied so that if one fails, another can seamlessly take over. This includes servers, storage systems,

and network paths. Data replication across availability zones or regions helps ensure business continuity.

2. **Monitoring and Alerting**: Constant monitoring is essential for detecting performance anomalies or outages. Alerting systems that notify operations staff about issues can significantly reduce Mean Time to Recovery (MTTR). Logs, metrics, and distributed tracing all contribute to a granular view of system health and help in diagnosing issues faster.

3. **Disaster Recovery**: Providers must have a disaster recovery (DR) plan outlining how the service will recover from worst-case scenarios like data center failures, natural disasters, or catastrophic security breaches. A comprehensive DR plan includes data backups, secondary data centers (hot, warm, or cold), and tested failover procedures.

4. **Continuous Testing**: High uptime targets require thorough, automated testing processes that run continuously. Testing should cover code changes, infrastructure updates, and failover scenarios to confirm that the environment can handle disruptions gracefully.

Balancing Performance and Cost

SaaS developers often need to strike a balance between providing high performance and controlling operational costs. Over-engineering a system can lead to inflated expenses with diminishing returns for actual business needs. Under-engineering can save money initially but result in dissatisfied customers and a tarnished reputation if performance or availability falters. Achieving the right balance involves data-driven decision-making, capacity planning, and iterative optimization, ensuring that resources match customer demands.

Chapter 2: Architectural Principles of SaaS

In the rapidly evolving domain of cloud computing, a robust understanding of architectural principles is vital for any organization looking to build or maintain SaaS solutions. An application's architecture underpins everything from how code is structured to how users experience performance during peak loads. Done right, a well-designed architecture not only ensures immediate functionality but also positions a product for long-term success, facilitating updates, scaling, and integrations with minimal friction.

SaaS, by its nature, demands architectural strategies that emphasize **multi-tenancy**, **resource efficiency**, **modularity**, and **constant evolution**. A single instance often serves multiple organizations (tenants) in a way that's transparent to each, while seamlessly handling potentially large and unpredictable workloads. The quest to satisfy myriad tenants under one logical umbrella—yet also offer a degree of customization—adds both complexity and opportunity. As we embark on this chapter, we'll explore these cornerstones of SaaS architecture in detail, starting with core architectural patterns, then moving into multi-tenancy models, and finally examining the all-important topic of designing for scalability.

2.1 Core Architectural Patterns

The foundational layer of any SaaS solution rests on one or more architectural patterns that dictate how functionality is composed, how data flows, and how updates are managed. Choosing an appropriate pattern (or combination of patterns) impacts not only the code structure but also how the system evolves under changing business requirements. Two patterns that frequently dominate the SaaS conversation are the **monolithic architecture** and the **microservices architecture**. While these two approaches often appear in contrast, each has its own strengths and limitations. Equally important is the concept of layering, which helps teams systematically separate concerns and manage complexity across large codebases.

2.1.1 Monolithic vs. Microservices

For many years, software was built as a **monolith**, meaning all components—user interface, data access layers, business logic, and third-party integrations—resided in one self-contained codebase and were deployed as a single unit. More recently, **microservices** have emerged as an alternative: small, focused services that each handle a specific function within a larger application ecosystem. While there's a tendency to think of monolithic and microservices architectures as diametrically opposed, both have valid use cases, and understanding their trade-offs is critical for anyone designing SaaS applications.

Monolithic Architecture: Overview and Suitability

A monolithic architecture bundles all aspects of a software application into one executable or deployment package. When developers build or release new versions, they compile and deploy this singular artifact to a server (or cluster of servers) that runs the entire system. Although monoliths have fallen out of favor in some corners of the software world—due in large part to the popularity of microservices—several attributes still make them attractive in certain SaaS scenarios:

1. **Simplified Deployment**: Because the application is deployed as a single unit, developers can avoid the complexities associated with managing numerous separate services. Deployment pipelines are often more straightforward, especially for small teams. This simplicity can be an advantage for early-stage startups that want to move quickly and have limited engineering resources.

2. **Ease of Local Development**: Running a monolith locally is typically simpler for a developer to set up, since the entire codebase resides in one repository, with a unified environment for dependencies. This can accelerate the onboarding process for new team members.

3. **Shared Models and Libraries**: All code resides in the same project, so developers don't need to worry about duplicating common models or utility libraries across services. There's no immediate need for inter-service contracts or complicated version negotiations.

4. **Established Tooling**: While microservices require specialized orchestration and monitoring solutions, monolithic architectures often fit well with existing, well-known frameworks that integrate the presentation layer, business logic, and data persistence into a single toolchain. This is especially true in ecosystems like Java's Spring Boot, Ruby on Rails, or ASP.NET MVC.

Despite these conveniences, monolithic architectures can become unwieldy as an application grows in complexity. A large codebase may develop tangled dependencies, making it risky or time-consuming to change or refactor certain functionalities. Moreover, scaling a monolith typically means replicating the entire application on new servers, even if only one module is experiencing heavy load. This coarse-grained approach to scalability can be cost-inefficient over time.

Hence, for SaaS teams, a monolith might be the right choice if the product is in its early stages, or if its scope is well-defined and unlikely to grow exponentially. Many successful SaaS products launched as monoliths and later migrated to microservices once they outgrew the single-bundle deployment model. The decision often boils down to balancing the immediate speed of development and deployment against potential future complexity.

Microservices Architecture: Overview and Suitability

In contrast to monoliths, a **microservices** architecture breaks an application into a set of discrete services, each responsible for a specific bounded context or domain function. For instance, in a SaaS e-commerce platform, you might have separate services for user management, orders, payments, analytics, and notifications. Each service can be deployed, scaled, and updated independently, which grants a remarkable degree of flexibility.

Key traits of microservices architectures include:

1. **Loosely Coupled Services**: Services communicate primarily through well-defined APIs (often REST, gRPC, or a messaging queue), reducing dependencies between them. This isolation means that a change in one service usually does not necessitate changes in others, provided the interface (API contract) remains consistent.

2. **Independent Deployment and Versioning**: Each service can have its own release cycle and technology stack. Teams responsible for a particular service can choose the programming languages, frameworks, and databases that best fit their component, as long as they respect the agreed-upon interface. This allows for polyglot programming within the same SaaS product.

3. **Fine-Grained Scalability**: Because services are decoupled, you can independently scale only those parts of the system experiencing heavy usage. For instance, if the analytics service requires additional processing power due to increasing data volume, you can add more instances of that service without touching the rest of the application.

4. **Fault Isolation**: If one service fails or experiences performance degradation, it may not bring down the entire application—provided you have designed your system with proper fallback and circuit breaker patterns. This can significantly improve the overall reliability of the SaaS offering.

5. **Organizational Alignment**: Microservices align well with larger, cross-functional teams. Each service can be owned by a small team that independently manages its roadmap and backlog. This fosters accountability and domain specialization within the team and can speed up iteration.

While microservices offer numerous benefits, they also introduce new complexities. For example, each service must handle its own data persistence, meaning your SaaS solution will have multiple databases or data stores to manage. Monitoring and debugging can become more challenging, as you need to trace requests across multiple services in a distributed environment. Network latency and reliability also play a bigger role in overall performance.

Deciding Factors in SaaS

For SaaS providers, the choice between monolithic and microservices architectures hinges on multiple factors. Below are a few guiding questions teams often consider:

- **Team Size and Skill Set**: Smaller teams may prefer a monolith to reduce overhead. Larger teams with varied expertise might find microservices more manageable.
- **Application Complexity**: If your SaaS solution has numerous subsystems that will grow or need to scale independently, microservices can be more sustainable. A simpler or more niche product may run just fine as a monolith indefinitely.
- **Time to Market**: Early-stage startups often need to deliver an MVP (Minimum Viable Product) quickly. A monolith can accelerate initial development. Over time, if the product gains traction, a structured approach to refactoring into microservices may become necessary.
- **Organizational Culture**: Microservices demand an investment in DevOps, continuous integration/continuous deployment (CI/CD), and operational excellence. If an organization is not prepared to handle the complexity of distributed systems and advanced tooling, a monolith might be more practical.
- **Scalability Requirements**: If your SaaS is likely to see rapid scaling needs in certain areas—like advanced analytics, real-time collaboration, or large data streams—planning for microservices from the outset can be beneficial. However, even a monolith can be scaled up to a certain extent with well-thought-out design optimizations.

Ultimately, many SaaS providers begin with a monolithic approach, enjoying the immediate simplicity and lower overhead. Once the product's success and complexity warrant it, they refactor or gradually decompose the monolith into discrete microservices. This phased evolution can offer the best of both worlds: speed in early development and organizational resilience later.

2.1.2 Layered Architecture in SaaS

In addition to the high-level debate around monolithic vs.

microservices, nearly all successful SaaS applications employ some form of **layered architecture**. The principle behind a layered architecture is to separate different areas of responsibility within the application into well-defined layers, each focusing on a specific set of tasks. By doing so, you enforce discipline in your codebase, reducing coupling and making the application more maintainable over time.

Typical Layers

While various layering schemes exist, a standard breakdown for SaaS (and most enterprise software) looks something like the following:

1. **Presentation Layer (or Interface Layer)**: This layer handles all user interactions, encompassing user interface logic, front-end components, and possibly an API gateway if you're exposing REST or GraphQL endpoints for external consumption. It focuses on rendering data to the user, gathering user input, and forwarding relevant requests to the next layer.

2. **Application Layer (or Service Layer)**: The application layer coordinates business operations, orchestrating data flow between various sub-components. Here you might find the core logic that validates requests, enforces business rules, and interacts with domain entities. In a microservices context, each service might have its own mini-application layer, or you can incorporate some domain logic here if the architecture is still monolithic.

3. **Domain/Business Logic Layer**: In certain layered approaches (particularly those influenced by **domain-driven design**), you might have a separate domain layer that holds the application's core business rules, entities, value objects, and domain services. By isolating the domain logic, you ensure that complex business operations remain unaffected by the intricacies of front-end or infrastructure concerns.

4. **Data Access Layer (or Persistence Layer)**: This layer interacts directly with the database or other storage mechanisms. It is responsible for CRUD (Create, Read, Update, Delete) operations and ensuring data consistency, possibly via object-relational mappers (ORMs) or other persistence frameworks. This separation reduces the risk of scattering data-related code across the application.

5. **Infrastructure Layer**: Some frameworks treat infrastructure as a distinct layer that encapsulates technical concerns such as messaging brokers, file storage, logging, caching, and external integrations (e.g., calling third-party APIs). This approach centralizes anything that might require specialized libraries or connections, keeping them abstracted from core business logic.

Even in a microservices environment, layering remains relevant. Each microservice can have its own internal layering, enabling clarity of responsibility and a strict boundary between its logic and external systems. As microservices communicate with each other via APIs, layering ensures that these communication points are well-defined and standardized.

Benefits of Layering

1. **Maintainability**: By segregating code according to function, developers can modify or refactor one layer without necessarily impacting the others. This structure helps keep the codebase clean, improving long-term maintainability.

2. **Testability**: Layered designs often enhance testability. For instance, you can mock the data access layer when testing business logic, or create unit tests for the domain layer that ignore the complexities of the UI or external services.

3. **Reusability**: Certain layers, like the domain and data access layers, can be reused in different contexts. For instance, you might develop a web interface, a mobile app, and a partner API, all referencing the same domain logic.

4. **Team Specialization**: In larger organizations, developers may specialize in front-end, back-end, or database concerns. Layering provides a clear structure for allocating work, ensuring that experts can focus on areas that leverage their strengths.

Common Pitfalls

While layered architecture is well-established, it can lead to inefficiencies if not applied properly:

- **Excessive Layer Hopping**: Over-engineering can happen if each request passes through too many abstraction layers with minimal logic in each. This can cause performance overhead and confusion about where logic truly belongs.

- **Vague Layer Boundaries**: If boundaries are not well-defined, one layer's logic can "bleed" into another. This is particularly dangerous in the business logic and data layers, where you might see direct database calls from what is supposed to be domain code.

- **Monolithic Tangle**: Layered architecture can become monolithic and bloated over time if multiple domain contexts are forced into the same set of layers without a clear separation or modularization strategy.

For SaaS, layering remains a best practice, regardless of whether you adopt monolithic or microservices approaches. The clarity of responsibilities, along with the facilitation of testing and maintenance, can be a deciding factor in whether the application can quickly adapt to new feature requests, business pivots, or evolving regulatory requirements. In subsequent chapters, you'll see how layering interacts with topics like data security, compliance, and advanced cloud deployments—yet the basic principle remains the same: separate concerns and keep your code well-organized.

2.2 Multi-Tenancy Models

Arguably the defining characteristic of SaaS—distinguishing it from traditional hosted applications—is the **multi-tenant** nature of the software. In a multi-tenant system, multiple organizations (or "tenants") share the same infrastructure and application codebase while keeping their data logically isolated. Implementing multi-tenancy efficiently and securely is a central challenge in SaaS architecture, as it impacts performance, cost, and how updates are rolled out.

2.2.1 Single-Tenant vs. Multi-Tenant Architectures

One way to conceptualize multi-tenancy is to compare it with **single-tenant** deployments:

- **Single-Tenant**: Each customer or tenant has its own dedicated instance of the software, often hosted in a separate environment. Configuration, data storage, and even some aspects of infrastructure usage can be isolated on a per-tenant basis. While this ensures robust data separation, it also multiplies the operational overhead—each tenant's instance has to be deployed, monitored, and updated separately.

- **Multi-Tenant**: A single codebase and infrastructure serve all tenants. Tenants typically have separate data partitions (handled in the database schema or at the application level), but they share the same underlying services and compute resources. This drastically simplifies deployment and maintenance, as updates can be rolled out to all tenants simultaneously. However, it also demands a more careful approach to security, data isolation, and resource allocation to ensure one tenant's usage doesn't degrade performance for the others.

Drivers Behind Multi-Tenant SaaS

SaaS providers often favor **multi-tenant** designs because of the following benefits:

1. **Economies of Scale**: By sharing resources, a provider can serve multiple customers on the same hardware. This reduces overall costs and can lead to competitive pricing that single-tenant hosting might not match.

2. **Centralized Maintenance**: With a shared codebase, updates and patches can be applied once for all tenants, streamlining release cycles. This is a significant efficiency gain over single-tenant models, where each customer's instance may need individual attention.

3. **Consistent User Experience**: While some level of customization is possible, multi-tenant platforms tend to keep everyone on a unified version of the software, ensuring consistency. This helps support teams and reduces the complexity of managing different feature sets across customers.

4. **Simplified Onboarding**: Provisioning a new tenant in a well-designed multi-tenant system often involves little more than creating entries in a database or assigning resources through an admin portal. Contrast that with single-tenant setups, which might require spinning up a new virtual machine or container environment for each additional customer.

Despite these advantages, some organizations—especially those with strict compliance requirements or specialized performance needs—may lean toward a single-tenant solution, where they have dedicated resources and a more controlled environment. Hybrid approaches also exist, in which a SaaS provider can offer multi-tenancy for most small and medium customers but allow premium enterprise clients to run in semi-isolated or fully single-tenant environments for an extra fee.

Key Considerations When Designing Multi-Tenant Systems

- **Tenant Isolation**: Ensuring that data and computations from different tenants do not leak into each other's domain is paramount. Tenant IDs, schema separation, and robust access control checks are common strategies.

- **Performance Consistency**: If one tenant significantly spikes usage, it can degrade performance for others. Solutions involve resource throttling, quality-of-service rules, or architectural designs that can quickly isolate or scale the affected services.

- **Customizability vs. Standardization**: Some tenants need specialized features or integrations. Balancing the desire for a standardized codebase with the flexibility to handle custom requirements can be challenging. Feature flags, plugin systems, and dedicated customization modules can help.

- **Billing and Metering**: Many SaaS offerings rely on usage-based pricing, which can be tricky in a multi-tenant environment. Accurate metering of resources consumed per tenant requires meticulous logging and reporting infrastructure.

2.2.2 Database Strategies for Multi-Tenancy

One of the most critical aspects of multi-tenant design is how you store and partition tenant data in the database layer. The chosen strategy can significantly affect performance, operational cost, and the ease of scaling. Below are the most common approaches:

1. **Shared Database, Shared Schema**:

   o **Description**: All tenants share the same database and the same set of tables. Tenant data is differentiated by a column that indicates which tenant a row belongs to (e.g., a tenant_id field).
   o **Benefits**:
      ▪ Simple to provision new tenants (insert rows for tenant definitions).
      ▪ Lowest hardware cost, as all data resides in one place.
      ▪ Centralized maintenance tasks (backups, indexing) applied to a single database.
   o **Drawbacks**:
      ▪ The highest risk if isolation is not carefully enforced—any query or code mistake can mix data across tenants.
      ▪ Large table sizes can eventually hamper performance if not optimized.
   o **Use Cases**: This is often the first choice for smaller SaaS providers who want to minimize infrastructure complexity and cost, or for products where each tenant's data volume is small.

2. **Shared Database, Separate Schemas**:

   o **Description**: All tenants share the same physical database server, but each tenant has its own logical schema (e.g., separate sets of tables named or namespaced according to the tenant).
   o **Benefits**:

- Clearer data isolation compared to a shared schema, as each tenant's data lives in separate tables.
- Easier to archive or move an individual tenant's data if needed.

○ **Drawbacks**:
- Still a single database instance, which can be a single point of failure or performance bottleneck.
- Over time, numerous schemas can become unwieldy. Database upgrades and migrations may be complex.

○ **Use Cases**: Ideal for SaaS where each tenant might have distinct data structures or significantly varied data volumes, but the provider still wants the convenience of a single database management environment.

3. **Separate Databases**:

○ **Description**: Each tenant has its own dedicated database (or database instance), though the application code might be identical across all tenants.

○ **Benefits**:
- The strongest logical isolation. Each tenant's data is fully contained, making compliance audits and data archiving more straightforward.
- Performance issues in one tenant's database are less likely to affect others (assuming resource contention at the server level is managed).

○ **Drawbacks**:
- Higher cost, as each tenant effectively needs a separate set of database resources.
- More complex to manage and monitor, especially as the number of tenants grows.
- Rolling out schema changes to numerous databases can be time-consuming.

- Use Cases: Common in B2B SaaS catering to large enterprises with stringent data isolation requirements, or in "hybrid" SaaS solutions where some critical or regulated clients demand single-tenant environments while others share resources.

4. **NoSQL or Sharded Approaches**:

  - **Description**: Instead of relational databases, some SaaS solutions use document stores (MongoDB, Couchbase), key-value stores, or wide-column databases (Cassandra) and store each tenant's data in separate collections, tables, or partitions. Additionally, sharding can distribute large datasets across multiple servers or clusters.
  - **Benefits**:
    - Highly scalable, handling large volumes of data or high transaction throughput.
    - Flexible data models can adapt to different tenants' needs without complex migrations.
  - **Drawbacks**:
    - Lack of relational integrity or complex query support in some NoSQL systems.
    - More specialized skill set required to manage and optimize.
  - **Use Cases**: SaaS products dealing with big data, real-time analytics, or unstructured data, where the application's data model is fluid and performance at scale is paramount.

Choosing among these database strategies involves trade-offs between cost, complexity, security, performance, and compliance. Many SaaS providers begin with a shared schema in a single database and later move to separate schemas or separate databases as their tenant base and data volumes grow. Some solutions adopt a hybrid approach, offering small clients a multi-tenant shared schema while providing larger clients with dedicated instances for better performance and data isolation.

2.3 Designing for Scalability

Scalability is a watchword in SaaS architecture, reflecting the fundamental need to accommodate growing workloads without sacrificing performance or stability. While future chapters delve deeper into performance optimization and monitoring, the conceptual backbone of scalability begins with architectural design. By planning for scale from the outset, SaaS teams can avoid painful refactors and last-minute overhauls once user demand begins to surge.

2.3.1 Horizontal and Vertical Scaling

When discussing scaling strategies, two key terms frequently emerge: **vertical scaling** and **horizontal scaling**.

Vertical Scaling (Scale-Up)

Vertical scaling entails increasing the computational capacity (CPU, RAM, storage) of a single server or node. For instance, if your SaaS runs on a virtual machine with 4 CPU cores and 16 GB of RAM, you might upgrade to 16 cores and 64 GB of RAM. This approach is sometimes called "scaling up" because you're making an existing instance more powerful.

- **Benefits**:

    1. **Simplicity**: Upgrading a server is often easier than redesigning your application to run on multiple nodes. You avoid additional overhead for distributing traffic or synchronizing data across multiple servers.
    2. **Consistency**: Because everything resides on a single node, you can keep the code structure simpler. There's

no need for distributed caching or complex load balancing.

3. **Potential Cost Savings (in Some Cases)**: Depending on the cloud provider's pricing structure, one larger machine may be cheaper than multiple smaller machines of comparable total capacity, though this is not always the case.

- **Drawbacks**:

  1. **Hardware Limits**: Eventually, you will hit the upper limit of hardware resources, whether due to technological constraints or provider-imposed maximums.
  2. **Single Point of Failure**: If your application lives on a single node, a failure in that node can mean a full outage, unless you have robust failover mechanisms.
  3. **Diminishing Returns**: As hardware resources scale, performance gains may not be linear due to concurrency bottlenecks in the application code or the operating system.

In a SaaS context, vertical scaling can suffice for early growth stages or for monolithic systems that haven't yet demanded the complexity of distributed computing. It can also complement horizontal scaling, especially if certain services are CPU or memory-intensive, but only if the architecture allows for it.

Horizontal Scaling (Scale-Out)

Horizontal scaling adds more servers or nodes to the infrastructure, distributing workloads among them. If one node gets overloaded, new instances can be spun up (often automatically) to handle additional traffic or computational demands. This is the essence of "scaling out."

- **Benefits**:

1. **Virtually Unlimited Growth**: In theory, you can keep adding more nodes as traffic increases, constrained primarily by your budget and how your application manages distributed data.
2. **Resilience**: With multiple nodes, you often gain fault tolerance. If one node fails, the load balancer can route requests to other healthy nodes, reducing downtime.
3. **Granular Scalability**: You can scale different components or services independently. If your analytics pipeline needs more processing power while your user-facing front end remains stable, you can add nodes specifically for analytics.

- **Drawbacks**:

1. **Complexity**: Managing multiple nodes requires load balancers, distributed caching, and data synchronization mechanisms. Operational overhead grows as the cluster expands.
2. **Consistency Challenges**: Data consistency can be harder to maintain across distributed nodes. Techniques like sharding, partitioning, or eventual consistency models might be needed.
3. **Network Overhead**: Communication among nodes introduces latency. In some heavily interactive workloads, network overhead might become a bottleneck.

For many SaaS applications, horizontal scaling is a core principle. It aligns well with microservices architectures, where individual services can be replicated based on demand. Modern cloud platforms also offer managed container orchestration (e.g., Kubernetes) and serverless approaches that simplify many aspects of horizontal scaling by automatically provisioning resources in response to usage patterns.

In practice, a robust SaaS architecture often employs a **hybrid** of vertical and horizontal scaling. Certain workloads are best addressed by adding more powerful machines (e.g., data-intensive processes that benefit from abundant RAM), while the bulk of the application is designed to scale horizontally to handle user traffic spikes.

2.3.2 Load Balancing Strategies

Load balancing is the linchpin that makes horizontal scaling viable. It distributes incoming requests across multiple application instances (or servers), ensuring no single node becomes a bottleneck. In a SaaS environment—particularly one with multi-tenancy—load balancing must account not only for volume but also for equitable distribution, tenant isolation (if needed), and real-time capacity changes.

Fundamentals of Load Balancing

A load balancer typically listens on a public-facing endpoint (e.g., https://app.exampleSaaS.com) and routes requests to the backend servers that actually process them. The load balancer can be configured with algorithms such as **round-robin**, **least connections**, or **IP hash** to determine which node should handle each incoming request.

- **Round-Robin**: Each node receives requests in a cyclical sequence. This is simple and often fair if each node is roughly identical in capacity and each request has a similar load profile.
- **Least Connections**: The balancer routes requests to the node currently handling the fewest active connections. This works well in scenarios with variable request-processing times.
- **IP Hash**: The client's IP address is hashed, and that hash determines which node will service the request. This can be beneficial if session affinity is needed (i.e., the same user session must consistently go to the same server).

SaaS solutions often require a more sophisticated approach, because they might need session persistence, SSL/TLS termination, or advanced routing rules that direct requests to specialized nodes. Some load balancers also perform health checks, removing any unresponsive servers from rotation and reintroducing them once they recover.

Layer 4 vs. Layer 7 Load Balancing

Load balancing can occur at different layers of the OSI model, often summarized as **Layer 4** (transport layer) and **Layer 7** (application layer). Understanding these distinctions helps in designing an effective SaaS architecture.

- **Layer 4 Load Balancing**: Operates at the network protocol level (TCP or UDP). The balancer routes traffic based on IP addresses and port numbers without inspecting the actual content of the packets. This approach is faster due to lower overhead but lacks nuanced control.
- **Layer 7 Load Balancing**: Operates at the application layer (e.g., HTTP), allowing the balancer to inspect the content of requests. This can enable routing decisions based on URLs, headers, or cookies. For SaaS, you might route requests for specific subdomains or feature sets to specialized service instances.

Layer 7 load balancers, often referred to as **application gateways**, are particularly useful in a SaaS environment that includes microservices. They can parse the request path, headers, or JWT tokens to decide which service should handle the request, supporting version-based routing or A/B testing. That said, the deeper the inspection, the higher the computational overhead for the load balancer, which might matter at scale.

Advanced Balancing Techniques for SaaS

1. **Global Load Balancing**: For SaaS providers with a global user base, load balancing can extend beyond a single region. Global load balancers or DNS-based load balancing can route

users to the nearest data center, reducing latency and balancing cross-region traffic.

2. **Tenant-Aware Routing**: In multi-tenant SaaS, certain large customers might have dedicated nodes or specialized performance requirements. A load balancer (especially at Layer 7) can detect the tenant via the request URL, token, or subdomain, then direct that customer's traffic to the assigned environment.

3. **Elastic Autoscaling**: Most modern cloud platforms support autoscaling groups or container orchestration that spin up new instances as metrics (e.g., CPU utilization or queue length) exceed thresholds. The load balancer automatically discovers and adds these new instances to its rotation, achieving near real-time scaling.

4. **Blue-Green or Canary Deployments**: When releasing new features, a load balancer can direct a small percentage of traffic to a "green" environment running the new version, while most traffic remains on the "blue" environment (the older, stable version). If no issues arise, the balancer gradually shifts more traffic to the new version. If problems surface, the balancer can revert traffic to the stable version. This approach reduces deployment risk and can be crucial in ensuring continuous, uninterrupted service in a SaaS product.

Balancing Cost, Complexity, and Reliability

Load balancing is fundamental to high availability and scalability, but each layer of balancing adds operational overhead and expense. Managed load balancers from major cloud providers (e.g., AWS Elastic Load Balancing, Google Cloud Load Balancing, or Azure Load Balancer) simplify configuration but may have usage-based fees. Self-managed solutions, like HAProxy or Nginx, offer flexibility yet require expertise to configure and monitor effectively.

SaaS providers typically adopt a balanced approach: they leverage a combination of managed services for core load balancing functionality while customizing aspects such as API gateways or tenant-aware routing. This ensures both reliability and the granular control needed to meet the diverse demands of multi-tenant applications.

Chapter 3: Cloud Infrastructure for SaaS

Cloud infrastructure lies at the heart of virtually every successful SaaS platform. While earlier chapters discussed high-level architectural principles, multi-tenancy, and the basics of the SaaS model, this chapter shifts our perspective to the foundational layer that enables all of these abstractions. A provider's choice of cloud platform—along with how they provision, configure, and manage that platform—can have far-reaching implications, including cost efficiency, reliability, scalability, and overall development velocity.

Operating in the cloud is about more than just spinning up virtual machines and storing data. It encompasses every aspect of application delivery, from automatically deploying compute resources to orchestrating networks, storage, security, and monitoring. For many SaaS providers, the cloud confers a competitive edge by offloading the complexities of physical hardware management, offering near-limitless global scale, and facilitating rapid deployment of new features. Yet each cloud platform and each approach to provisioning has unique strengths and trade-offs.

Throughout this chapter, we will walk step-by-step through the core concepts of cloud infrastructure for SaaS:

1. **Choosing the Right Cloud Provider** – We will examine major players like AWS, Microsoft Azure, and Google Cloud Platform (GCP), delve into their distinguishing features, and explore ways to factor cost into your decision.
2. **Infrastructure as Code (IaC)** – We will discuss how tools like Terraform and AWS CloudFormation can automate the provisioning and lifecycle management of cloud resources. Best practices for building robust, version-controlled, and repeatable infrastructure will be highlighted.
3. **Serverless Computing in SaaS** – We will investigate when and how serverless architectures fit into a SaaS strategy, including guidelines for choosing serverless services, analyzing benefits, and noting potential limitations.

By the end of this chapter, you will be equipped with a foundational understanding of how to effectively run SaaS in the cloud, make strategic decisions regarding providers and tooling, and harness modern deployment patterns to keep your application agile and cost-effective.

3.1 Choosing the Right Cloud Provider

Selecting a cloud provider is one of the earliest—and often most consequential—decisions you will make in building a SaaS product. In essence, a provider's service offerings, geographical reach, ecosystem maturity, and pricing structures can shape the success, limitations, and trajectory of your platform. While Amazon Web Services (AWS), Microsoft Azure, and Google Cloud Platform (GCP) dominate the space, there are also niche providers (DigitalOcean, Linode, Vultr, among others) that cater to specific needs.

This section details how to weigh various factors when evaluating providers, focusing on AWS, Azure, and GCP as representative examples. We will also explore the topic of cost—a crucial but often misunderstood component of cloud adoption. Keep in mind that no single provider is best for every scenario; each excels in certain areas, and the "best" choice depends on your target audience, application demands, compliance requirements, and budget constraints.

3.1.1 AWS, Azure, and Google Cloud Comparison

Amazon Web Services (AWS)

Launched in 2006, AWS is the largest and most mature public cloud provider. It leads the market in the breadth of services offered, supporting everything from on-demand compute (Amazon EC2) and managed Kubernetes (Amazon EKS) to fully managed big data pipelines (Amazon EMR, AWS Glue) and specialized machine learning platforms (Amazon SageMaker). AWS's major advantages include:

1. **Vast Ecosystem**: AWS has cultivated an extensive partner network and community. This means you'll find plenty of third-party integrations, prebuilt solutions on the AWS Marketplace, and user-generated content—such as blogs and tutorials—that tackle common architectural patterns.

2. **Global Reach**: AWS data centers (organized into Regions and Availability Zones) span the globe, enabling you to deploy SaaS solutions close to your customers. Services like Amazon Route 53 and AWS Global Accelerator also help streamline international traffic routing.

3. **Service Depth**: AWS not only has a wide array of services but each service often has multiple configurations or modes. For instance, in storage alone, you have Amazon S3 for object storage, Amazon EBS for block storage, Amazon EFS for file storage, and Amazon FSx for specialized file systems. Such depth can be overwhelming, but it allows you to fine-tune

48

solutions for unique performance or compliance requirements.

4. **Innovation Pace**: AWS frequently rolls out new services and features. While this keeps the platform at the cutting edge, it can also lead to a steeper learning curve as you attempt to keep up with frequent updates.

The main potential drawbacks of AWS include a relatively complex pricing model—navigating usage tiers, data transfer costs, and per-request pricing can be intimidating for newcomers—and a certain "tool sprawl" that can complicate architectural decision-making. Nonetheless, AWS remains a strong option for those seeking proven, enterprise-grade capabilities and a robust global footprint.

Microsoft Azure

Microsoft Azure (launched in 2010) has quickly grown into a formidable cloud platform, leveraging Microsoft's longstanding enterprise customer base, developer tools, and partnerships. Key strengths include:

1. **Enterprise Integration**: Azure integrates seamlessly with existing Microsoft technologies such as Active Directory, Windows Server, and the .NET ecosystem. If your SaaS solutions or customers rely heavily on Windows-based workloads or Office 365, Azure can provide a more unified experience.

2. **Hybrid Cloud Approach**: Azure's strength in hybrid cloud scenarios is unmatched. Services like Azure Arc and Azure Stack let you extend cloud capabilities to on-premises data centers or edge locations. This is especially valuable for large enterprises undergoing gradual cloud migrations or requiring data residency in specific locations.

3. **DevOps and Tooling**: Azure DevOps (formerly Visual Studio Team Services) and GitHub (acquired by Microsoft in 2018) facilitate a broad range of developer workflows and continuous integration/continuous deployment (CI/CD) pipelines. Azure also integrates well with third-party toolchains, but the synergy with Microsoft's products is particularly robust.

4. **AI and Analytics**: Like AWS, Azure offers a range of AI and big data services, including Azure Machine Learning, Azure Databricks, and Azure Synapse Analytics. These can be leveraged to build advanced analytics or data-driven SaaS solutions without heavy investments in your own data engineering.

On the downside, Azure's user interface and some services have a reputation for complexity or occasional inconsistency, stemming in part from the platform's rapid evolution. Additionally, while Azure's global presence is strong, it may have fewer regions in some parts of the world than AWS. Cost structures can be equally intricate, so due diligence in cost planning remains essential.

Google Cloud Platform (GCP)

GCP (announced in 2008 but heavily expanded in the mid-2010s) is a relatively smaller player in terms of market share but is favored by many SaaS startups for its simplicity, Google-grade infrastructure, and cutting-edge services in data analytics and machine learning. Notable advantages include:

1. **Kubernetes Leadership**: Google invented Kubernetes, the open-source container orchestration platform, and GCP's Google Kubernetes Engine (GKE) is considered by many to be the gold standard for managed Kubernetes. This can be a key differentiator if your SaaS relies heavily on container-based microservices.

2. **Machine Learning and Big Data**: GCP is renowned for its data analytics services (BigQuery, Dataflow, Dataproc) and machine learning tools (AutoML, Vertex AI). If your SaaS platform requires advanced predictive analytics or real-time data processing, GCP's offerings in this domain can be compelling.

3. **Simplified Interface and Developer Experience**: Many developers cite GCP's more streamlined interface and straightforward product lineup as easier to adopt. Fewer overlapping services can reduce confusion, making it friendlier for teams new to the cloud.

4. **Cost Innovations**: GCP introduced features like per-second billing early on, as well as automatic sustained-use discounts. This can simplify cost management and sometimes lead to lower bills compared to other providers, depending on your workloads.

Conversely, GCP's global footprint is not as extensive as AWS or Azure, which can matter if you need data centers in specific geographical regions or want maximum coverage for a worldwide user base. Additionally, while GCP has grown its enterprise features over time, some organizations still perceive it as more startup-oriented.

Other Providers

While AWS, Azure, and GCP dominate, smaller or specialized cloud providers like DigitalOcean, Vultr, and Linode can sometimes be attractive for simpler SaaS workloads or developer-friendly experiences. They often provide straightforward pricing, strong customer support, and ease of use. However, they might lack advanced services (like fully managed AI/ML, event streaming, or globally distributed SQL databases), and their data center footprint can be more limited.

In short, choosing a provider depends on criteria like ecosystem support, compliance requirements, existing tech stacks, global presence, cost considerations, and developer experience. Many SaaS companies start with one primary cloud platform and expand or adopt multi-cloud strategies only after they have a stable product-market fit.

3.1.2 Cost Considerations in Cloud Deployment

Cloud computing is often touted for its pay-as-you-go flexibility, allowing businesses to pay only for what they use. However, it is equally easy to accumulate unexpected costs if you don't actively monitor resource usage and optimize your infrastructure. This section offers an overview of key cost considerations specific to SaaS, along with tips for ensuring you achieve cost efficiency without sacrificing performance or customer satisfaction.

1. Understanding the Pricing Models

Most major cloud providers break down costs into a handful of categories:

- **Compute Costs**: Instances (virtual machines), containers, serverless function invocations, or managed service charges for resources like AWS Fargate or Azure Container Instances.
- **Storage and Database Costs**: Fees for storing data in object storage, block storage, or managed databases, often priced per gigabyte per month. Database services (like Amazon RDS, Azure SQL Database, or Cloud SQL) may also charge for compute and memory.
- **Networking and Data Transfer**: Fees for data transfer out to the public internet, inter-region transfers, or traffic flowing between availability zones or services. Some providers also charge differently for inbound vs. outbound data.
- **Managed Services**: Specialized offerings like data warehousing, AI/ML, search indexes, event streaming, or

message queues. Each typically has its own pricing model, e.g., per million requests, per node hour, or per partition used.

- **Support Plans**: Enterprise-level support from providers often comes with monthly fees based on a percentage of your overall cloud spending. This may be required for mission-critical or regulated workloads that need high levels of support availability.

2. Common Cost Pitfalls

Even with a solid grasp of pricing models, certain pitfalls are easy to overlook:

- **Over-Provisioning**: Teams may launch overly large VM instances or keep them running 24/7 when usage is sporadic. In a SaaS product, you can mitigate this with auto-scaling groups or serverless architectures that match resource usage to actual demand.
- **Zombie Resources**: Unused resources (idle VMs, stale data snapshots, or forgotten load balancers) can quietly rack up monthly bills. Regular "housekeeping" scans and resource tagging policies help reduce wasted spend.
- **Data Egress Costs**: Many teams forget how quickly data transfer charges add up. If your SaaS streams large data sets to customers or if you replicate data across regions, keep a close eye on egress fees.
- **Misaligned Storage Tiers**: Storing infrequently accessed data in premium tiers (like SSD-based block storage or nearline object storage) can spike costs without any noticeable performance benefit. Lifecycle policies that automatically move older data to cheaper tiers help address this issue.
- **Third-Party Services**: SaaS architectures often integrate with third-party APIs or rely on specialized providers for logging, alerting, or content delivery. Some of these services operate on

subscription or per-request models that can balloon if your traffic grows unexpectedly.

3. Strategies for Cost Optimization

Maximizing cost efficiency in the cloud is a continuous effort rather than a one-time exercise. Below are a few proven strategies:

1. **Right-Sizing and Auto-Scaling**: Monitor real-time metrics for CPU, memory, and network utilization. Adjust instance sizes or container resource limits accordingly. Implement auto-scaling groups that spin up or down resources based on usage thresholds.

2. **Reserved Instances or Savings Plans**: If your SaaS workload exhibits steady, predictable traffic, consider purchasing reserved instances or savings plans. These typically grant steep discounts in exchange for a commitment to a particular usage level or time period (e.g., one year or three years).

3. **Spot or Preemptible Instances**: AWS Spot Instances or GCP Preemptible VMs allow you to bid on spare capacity at significantly reduced rates—up to 90% cheaper than on-demand instances. The trade-off is that the provider can reclaim these instances at short notice if demand rises. This can still be cost-effective for non-critical or fault-tolerant workloads (e.g., background batch jobs, ephemeral CI/CD tasks).

4. **Storage Tiering**: Analyze data access patterns, then configure lifecycle rules to move older or less frequently accessed data to cheaper storage classes. For example, store "hot" data that needs millisecond retrieval in a standard tier, and move archived data to a cold storage tier.

5. **Continuous Monitoring and Alerts**: Tools like AWS Cost Explorer, Azure Cost Management, or GCP's Billing reports can break down expenses by service, region, or tag. Set cost alarms to catch unusual spikes early, and review monthly or weekly cost breakdowns to spot negative trends.

6. **Leverage Provider-Specific Credits**: Many providers offer startup credits or trial periods that can offset initial infrastructure costs. This can be especially beneficial for new SaaS products that want to test architecture or run proofs of concept before paying full price.

7. **FinOps Culture**: The emerging domain of Financial Operations (FinOps) encourages collaboration between engineering, finance, and product teams to control and optimize cloud spending. Establish clear accountability and share real-time cost data internally so stakeholders can make informed decisions about resource allocation.

Ultimately, cost optimization is not about penny-pinching at the expense of reliability or performance—especially in SaaS, where a subpar user experience can quickly erode trust. Instead, it's about running a lean, efficient infrastructure that can expand as your tenant base grows, while avoiding unneeded overhead. By establishing best practices early, you'll build a strong foundation for sustainable, scalable success in the cloud.

3.2 Infrastructure as Code (IaC)

Running SaaS in the cloud generally entails provisioning and managing an array of resources—compute instances, load balancers, databases, security groups, virtual networks, container registries, and more. In the early days of public cloud adoption, teams often created and managed these resources manually via web consoles or ad hoc scripts. As the scale and complexity of cloud deployments grew, such manual efforts quickly became error-prone and difficult to reproduce. **Infrastructure as Code (IaC)** emerged to address these challenges, enabling teams to define and manage infrastructure using declarative or imperative code, version control systems, and automated pipelines.

3.2.1 Tools: Terraform, AWS CloudFormation

A variety of IaC tools exist, each with its own philosophy and scope. Two of the most popular are **Terraform** (by HashiCorp) and **AWS CloudFormation**. While each serves a similar fundamental purpose—provisioning cloud resources in a repeatable, automated fashion—differences exist in syntax, multi-cloud support, and design approach.

Terraform

- **Provider-Agnostic**: Terraform is designed to work across multiple cloud providers and on-premises solutions, such as AWS, Azure, GCP, VMware, OpenStack, and many others. This multi-cloud support can be a major advantage if your SaaS product needs or plans to span more than one environment.

- **Declarative Configuration**: Terraform uses a declarative language (HashiCorp Configuration Language, or HCL), wherein you describe the desired state of resources. Terraform's engine then calculates the necessary steps to achieve that state, creating or modifying resources as needed. It also supports an execution plan feature, which shows you what changes will occur before actually applying them.

- **State Management**: Terraform keeps track of resource states in a local or remote state file. This file is essential for reconciling actual cloud resources with the configuration you've declared. For collaborative environments, teams commonly store state in a remote backend (e.g., AWS S3, Terraform Cloud) to avoid drift or conflicts.

- **Modules and Reusability**: Terraform promotes the idea of modules—reusable configurations that can be shared internally or publicly through the Terraform Registry. Modules simplify repetitive tasks and encourage best practices by encapsulating resource definitions (e.g., a standard network stack, a multi-tenant database cluster, or a containerized microservice environment).

- **Challenges**: While Terraform's multi-cloud support is powerful, it can sometimes lag behind the latest features introduced by specific providers. Teams must carefully manage state files, especially in large-scale or multi-team setups, to avoid collisions or partial updates. Additionally, debugging is not always as intuitive as in single-vendor tools.

Despite these challenges, Terraform is widely adopted due to its portability, strong community support, and relative ease of use once the basic concepts are mastered. For SaaS providers that want the freedom to use the best services across different clouds or avoid lock-in, Terraform is often the preferred choice.

AWS CloudFormation

- **AWS-Specific**: CloudFormation is AWS's native IaC service. It provides a way to define AWS resources in either JSON or YAML templates and automatically orchestrates their creation, update, and deletion. Because it's an AWS-owned service, it often has first-party support for new AWS features soon after launch.

- **Stack Concept**: In CloudFormation, a collection of AWS resources is grouped into a "stack." You can create, update, or delete stacks through the CloudFormation console, AWS CLI, or APIs. Each stack has a set of parameters, outputs, and a defined template referencing AWS services (EC2, S3, IAM, etc.).

- **Drift Detection**: CloudFormation includes a feature called drift detection, which checks if any resources have been manually modified outside of the stack's template. This helps you maintain consistency and avoid hidden configuration changes.

- **Nested Stacks and StackSets**: CloudFormation supports nested stacks (reusable templates composed within a parent stack) to help break down large templates. Additionally, AWS StackSets let you deploy stacks across multiple AWS accounts and regions, a critical feature for enterprises that adopt a multi-account strategy for isolation or compliance.

- **Challenges**: Because CloudFormation is AWS-specific, moving or expanding to other cloud providers using the same templates is not possible. Also, while CloudFormation is powerful, some developers find the YAML/JSON syntax verbose and less flexible than HCL. Templates can grow quite large, and debugging can be cumbersome if error messages are not clear.

For SaaS platforms that are all-in on AWS, CloudFormation can be a natural choice. It offers tight integration with the AWS ecosystem, including support for many AWS-specific advanced features and less overhead in managing credentials or provider plugins. For multi-cloud or hybrid scenarios, Terraform is typically the more pragmatic option.

Other IaC Tools

Although Terraform and CloudFormation dominate the conversation, many other tools exist:

- **Azure Resource Manager (ARM) / Bicep**: The Microsoft Azure equivalent of CloudFormation. Bicep is a domain-specific language that aims to simplify Azure resource definitions.
- **Pulumi**: A tool that allows you to write infrastructure in general-purpose programming languages (TypeScript, Python, Go, C#), bridging the gap between developers and operations teams.
- **Chef, Puppet, Ansible**: Historically, these tools were more about configuration management at the operating system level. However, many have expanded to include cloud resource provisioning, though typically not as feature-rich in that domain as Terraform or native cloud IaC offerings.

3.2.2 Best Practices for Automated Infrastructure

Adopting IaC is more than installing a tool. It involves changes in workflow, development culture, and organizational practices. The best practices below help ensure a seamless and efficient DevOps pipeline:

1. **Version Control Everything**: Just like application source code, your infrastructure configurations should be stored in a Git repository (or equivalent). This practice ensures auditability (who changed what, when, and why) and facilitates rollback to known good states if a deployment fails.

2. **Use Separate Environments**: Maintain distinct environments (development, staging, production) with separate IaC configurations or environment-specific parameter files. This approach lets you test infrastructure changes in a safe environment before promoting them to production.

3. **Modularize Configurations**: Break down your IaC code into modules, each responsible for a logical set of resources (e.g., networking module, database module, identity and access

management module). This approach prevents large monolithic templates that are difficult to maintain or reuse.

4. **Incorporate Automated Testing**: Infrastructure testing can include linting your IaC files, validating syntax, running policy-as-code checks (e.g., using tools like HashiCorp Sentinel or Open Policy Agent), and even performing integration tests in a temporary environment. Automated tests reduce the likelihood of misconfigurations that can lead to outages or security vulnerabilities.

5. **Continuous Integration/Continuous Deployment (CI/CD)**: Combine IaC with a CI/CD pipeline to automatically validate changes on every pull request and automatically deploy to designated environments once changes are approved. This approach fosters a rapid feedback loop and ensures that infrastructure evolves predictably alongside application features.

6. **State Management and Locking**: If using a tool like Terraform, consider a remote backend (e.g., AWS S3 with DynamoDB locking) that enforces concurrency control. This prevents two engineers from updating the same infrastructure at the same time, which can cause conflicts or partial deployments.

7. **Secret Management**: Never store sensitive information (API keys, database passwords) directly in version control. Instead, reference them from a secure vault (e.g., AWS Secrets Manager, Azure Key Vault, or HashiCorp Vault). This ensures credentials remain protected while still being accessible during automated provisioning.

8. **Documentation and Onboarding**: Document how your IaC is structured, how modules are intended to be used, and the policies for merging changes. Publish short guides for new team members describing environment setups and the approval process for infrastructure modifications.

When your SaaS platform is fully realized as code, you gain the benefits of traceability, repeatability, and reduced human error. The net effect is that your infrastructure can evolve nearly as quickly as your application logic, unlocking true agility in responding to new business requirements or scaling needs.

3.3 Serverless Computing in SaaS

Serverless computing has taken the cloud world by storm, promising to abstract away server management entirely. Rather than provisioning, patching, and scaling your own virtual machines or containers, you simply upload small units of code (functions) or containerized services to a managed platform. The cloud provider automatically runs these functions in response to triggers, scales them horizontally, and charges you only for actual usage. This model can be especially powerful for SaaS architectures that have variable workloads, event-driven logic, or requirements for rapid development cycles.

3.3.1 When to Use Serverless Architecture

While serverless can be appealing, it's crucial to understand the use cases for which it is best suited. Some SaaS teams embrace serverless wholeheartedly, building entire applications around it, while others use it more selectively as part of a hybrid strategy.

1. Event-Driven Workloads

Serverless excels at handling event-driven workloads—such as responding to a user action, processing a queue, or reacting to a database update. In a SaaS environment, you might use serverless functions to:

- Resize images whenever a tenant uploads a profile picture.
- Validate incoming data streams and write them to the appropriate storage.
- Trigger push notifications or emails when a specific business event occurs.
- Perform asynchronous tasks like invoice generation or reporting, which can operate in the background.

Because these tasks might not run continuously, a serverless approach eliminates the cost and overhead of maintaining idle servers.

2. Infrequent or Spiky Demand

In multi-tenant SaaS, some features may be used only occasionally, or usage patterns can have massive spikes—for instance, if many tenants generate month-end reports at the same time. Serverless computing automatically scales to meet these demands, enabling your system to handle sudden bursts of traffic without requiring manual intervention or the constant expense of peak capacity. Once the surge is over, the environment scales back down, lowering costs.

3. Rapid Prototyping and Iteration

Serverless development can accelerate the software lifecycle. Developers can push new functions quickly, focusing on business logic rather than infrastructure details. Built-in integrations—for instance, AWS Lambda's direct connectivity to S3 or DynamoDB, or Azure Functions' triggers for Cosmos DB or Event Hub—further streamline the creation of event-driven workflows. If your SaaS product is in fast iteration mode, where small, frequent releases are critical, serverless can offer a compelling productivity boost.

4. Microservices and Polyglot Environments

Because serverless platforms typically support multiple languages (Node.js, Python, Go, C#, Java, etc.), you can adopt a polyglot approach where each function is written in the language that best suits its logic. This approach aligns with microservices patterns, though on an even smaller scale. Each service or function is isolated in its own environment, scaling independently of others.

3.3.2 Benefits and Limitations

Benefits

1. **No Server Management**: Arguably the biggest draw, serverless computing offloads the patching, load balancing, and capacity planning to the cloud provider. You focus solely on writing and deploying code.

2. **Cost Efficiency**: Pay-per-execution pricing ensures you pay only for actual invocations, usually billed in milliseconds of execution time. This can be a game-changer for sporadic or unpredictable workloads that would otherwise require expensive, always-on servers.

3. **Built-In Scalability**: Serverless platforms automatically spin up more function instances to meet demand, then spin them down when traffic subsides. This fosters near-instant horizontal scaling.

4. **Integration Ecosystem**: Most serverless platforms seamlessly integrate with other managed services. For instance, AWS Lambda can be triggered by SQS, EventBridge, or API Gateway; Azure Functions can be triggered by Azure Service Bus or Event Grid; Google Cloud Functions can be triggered by Pub/Sub or Firebase events. This reduces boilerplate and simplifies event-driven designs.

5. **Ease of Deployment**: Deploying serverless functions can be as simple as using a CLI or integrating into your CI/CD pipeline. Many frameworks (Serverless Framework, AWS SAM, Claudia.js) abstract away details and streamline development.

Limitations

1. **Cold Starts**: When a serverless function is not running, the platform must initialize a new runtime environment upon invocation. This "cold start" can introduce latency of hundreds of milliseconds (or more) for the first request after idle time. While providers have mitigated this over time (offering features like AWS Lambda Provisioned Concurrency), it remains a concern for low-latency applications.

2. **Execution Time and Memory Limits**: Serverless platforms impose limits on how long a function can run (e.g., 15 minutes for AWS Lambda) and how much memory it can consume (e.g., up to 10GB for Lambda). Complex or long-running jobs might exceed these limits, necessitating a different architecture.

3. **Distributed Complexity**: Breaking an application into dozens (or hundreds) of functions can lead to complicated inter-service communications. Observability, logging, and debugging can be more challenging, as traces must span ephemeral function instances. You must adopt robust logging, distributed tracing, and error-handling patterns.

4. **Vendor Lock-In**: Serverless offerings typically rely heavily on a provider's ecosystem of triggers and integrations. If you build extensively around AWS Lambda or Azure Functions, migrating to another platform can be labor-intensive.

5. **Pricing Surprises**: While pay-per-execution is often beneficial, some scenarios can lead to unexpectedly high costs—e.g., a function that's invoked excessively due to a poorly handled event or infinite loop. Monitoring usage metrics and setting up alerts is critical.

Use Cases Within SaaS

Serverless can be particularly effective in certain SaaS contexts. For instance, a multi-tenant analytics module might use serverless functions to transform large data sets into summarized reports. Or a communications module could rely on serverless to handle inbound webhooks from various third-party integrations, scaling seamlessly during peak inbound traffic. Meanwhile, stable core functionality with predictable usage might still reside on containerized or VM-based environments. This hybrid model ensures you leverage the best of both worlds: the cost-savings and elasticity of serverless for asynchronous or event-driven tasks, and the consistency and control of managed compute for core interactive services.

Chapter 4: Data Management in SaaS

Data is the lifeblood of any SaaS application. As a platform grows and serves a diverse multi-tenant user base, managing data efficiently becomes paramount. In this chapter, we examine the core strategies and best practices for designing, scaling, and maintaining databases in a SaaS environment. We explore schema design considerations, methods for scaling databases to meet fluctuating workloads, approaches to partitioning and sharding data, and finally, strategies for caching to enhance performance and reduce latency. By mastering these topics, architects and developers can ensure that their SaaS offerings deliver rapid, consistent, and secure data access regardless of scale.

Data management in SaaS is particularly challenging because it must support multi-tenancy while isolating and protecting each customer's data. Moreover, a SaaS provider must be ready to handle rapid growth, unpredictable usage patterns, and increasing volumes of transactional and analytical data. In what follows, we delve into each layer of data management, offering practical guidance, technical insights, and detailed examples to help you design a robust, scalable data management strategy that aligns with your SaaS business goals.

4.1 Database Design for SaaS

A well-thought-out database design is the cornerstone of a high-performing SaaS application. Given that many SaaS platforms operate in multi-tenant environments, your database architecture must balance the need for data isolation with the efficiencies of resource sharing. In this section, we examine the key considerations in designing a database schema for SaaS, as well as strategies to scale the database as your user base and data volume grow.

4.1.1 Schema Design Considerations

Understanding Multi-Tenancy in Data Models

When designing a schema for SaaS applications, one of the first questions you must answer is: how will you support multi-tenancy? There are several approaches:

- **Shared Schema with Tenant Identifiers:** In many SaaS solutions, a single database schema is shared among all tenants. Each table includes a tenant identifier (e.g., tenant_id) to isolate data. This model maximizes resource efficiency because a single set of tables serves all customers. However, it demands rigorous query design and access control to ensure that data from one tenant is never exposed to another.

  For example, every query must include a filter like WHERE tenant_id = ? to guarantee proper data isolation.

- **Separate Schemas:** An alternative approach is to maintain separate schemas within the same database instance for each tenant. This method enhances data isolation, making it simpler to enforce security boundaries. The downside is the increased complexity in managing many schemas, especially as the number of tenants grows. Automated tools and naming conventions become essential in this scenario.

67

- **Isolated Databases:** In environments where data security and performance are of paramount concern—such as in financial or healthcare applications—each tenant might be allocated a separate database instance. This approach maximizes isolation and can simplify compliance with industry regulations. However, isolated databases can drive up infrastructure costs and complicate global updates across tenants.

Normalization vs. Denormalization

Another key decision in schema design is choosing between normalization and denormalization. Each approach has its merits:

- **Normalization:** Normalization involves breaking data into multiple related tables to eliminate redundancy and ensure data integrity. Normalized schemas simplify updates and reduce storage costs. They are often preferred for transactional systems where data consistency is critical. However, heavy normalization may lead to complex join queries, which can hamper performance in high-read environments.

- **Denormalization:** Denormalization, in contrast, involves combining data into fewer tables to minimize the number of joins required during data retrieval. This approach is particularly beneficial for read-heavy workloads where performance and speed are prioritized. In a SaaS context, denormalization must be balanced carefully with data integrity concerns, often requiring additional logic in the application layer to maintain consistency.

For SaaS applications, the choice between normalization and denormalization often depends on the workload characteristics. Transactional modules (like order processing or user authentication) might benefit from a normalized schema, whereas reporting or analytics modules could see significant performance gains from a denormalized approach.

Flexible and Extensible Schemas

SaaS platforms frequently evolve as new features are added or customer requirements change. As a result, designing a schema that can accommodate future modifications without major rewrites is essential. Consider the following strategies:

- **Schema Versioning:** Implement version control for your database schema. Tools such as Liquibase or Flyway allow you to apply incremental changes, roll back modifications if necessary, and maintain a clear history of schema evolution. This is particularly important when multiple teams work on the same application.

- **Metadata-Driven Design:** Build flexibility into your schema by using metadata tables. For instance, instead of hard-coding every attribute of an entity, you might store attributes in a key-value pair format, allowing custom fields to be added without altering the primary table structure. This approach can be useful in multi-tenant scenarios where each customer might require unique data fields.

- **Polymorphic Associations:** When an entity can be associated with multiple types of related data, polymorphic associations can simplify the design. For example, if you have a "notes" table that might be attached to different entities (users, orders, support tickets), a polymorphic association allows you to store the type of the related entity along with its ID in a single table.

Security and Data Isolation Considerations

No matter how you choose to structure your schema, security must be a top priority. Data breaches in a SaaS environment can have catastrophic consequences. Here are some best practices:

- **Tenant-Aware Queries:** Every query must incorporate mechanisms to enforce tenant isolation. Beyond the simple use of a tenant_id column, consider implementing middleware layers that automatically inject tenant filters into queries.

- **Row-Level Security:** Many modern database systems offer row-level security features. This enables you to define security policies that ensure only authorized users can access specific rows, adding an extra layer of protection.

- **Encryption:** Data should be encrypted both at rest and in transit. Use database features and external encryption libraries to protect sensitive information. For multi-tenant environments, consider encrypting tenant-specific data with unique keys to prevent unauthorized cross-tenant data access.

- **Audit Trails:** Implement logging and audit trails to monitor data access and modifications. Audit logs can help detect unauthorized access, facilitate compliance reporting, and support forensic investigations in the event of a breach.

Balancing Performance and Maintainability

Ultimately, schema design must strike a balance between performance, maintainability, and security. A schema that is too rigid may hinder future growth, while one that is too flexible might introduce performance overhead. Consider the following:

- **Indexing Strategies:** Proper indexing is crucial for query performance, especially in multi-tenant databases. However, over-indexing can slow down write operations. Analyze query patterns carefully and adopt dynamic indexing strategies based on actual usage.
- **Caching Hot Data:** In many SaaS applications, a small subset of data is queried repeatedly. Strategically caching hot data at

the database or application level can significantly reduce load and improve response times.

- **Materialized Views:** For reporting and analytics, materialized views can pre-aggregate data and serve complex queries rapidly. They reduce the computational overhead on the main transactional tables while keeping the performance impact minimal.

By carefully considering these factors, you can craft a schema that is both performant and adaptable—ensuring that as your SaaS platform evolves, your data architecture evolves with it.

4.1.2 Scaling Databases for SaaS Applications

As your SaaS application scales, your database must be designed to accommodate increasing loads without sacrificing performance. Scalability challenges in data management include handling higher transaction volumes, managing larger data sets, and ensuring that complex queries return results in a timely manner. This section explores the strategies and best practices for scaling databases in a SaaS environment.

Vertical Scaling (Scale-Up) for Databases

Vertical scaling involves upgrading the hardware resources of a single database server—such as adding more CPU, memory, or faster storage—to handle higher loads. This method is often the simplest way to improve performance in the short term. However, vertical scaling has its limits:

- **Advantages of Vertical Scaling:** Vertical scaling can be implemented quickly and with minimal changes to the application. It often involves moving to a larger instance class or upgrading the storage subsystem to a faster, more robust option (for example, moving from magnetic drives to SSDs).

71

For SaaS platforms that experience gradual growth or have periodic spikes, vertical scaling may be sufficient for a while.

- **Limitations of Vertical Scaling:** Every machine has a finite capacity, and eventually, the workload will outgrow even the most powerful hardware. Moreover, vertical scaling does not address the inherent need for fault tolerance. If the single database instance fails, all tenants are affected. For these reasons, vertical scaling is often a temporary measure while preparing for more distributed solutions.

Horizontal Scaling (Scale-Out) for Databases

Horizontal scaling involves distributing the database load across multiple servers or instances. This approach can theoretically support near-infinite growth, as you can add more nodes to the system as needed. There are several techniques for horizontal scaling:

- **Replication:** Database replication involves maintaining copies of the same data on multiple servers. One common configuration is the master-slave (or primary-secondary) model, where the master handles writes and replicates changes to one or more slaves that serve read requests. This can greatly improve read performance and provide redundancy. However, replication introduces challenges with eventual consistency and may complicate write operations if the workload is write-heavy.

- **Sharding:** Sharding involves partitioning the data across multiple databases, each responsible for a subset of the data. In a SaaS environment, sharding can be done based on tenant identifiers (i.e., assigning different tenants to different shards) or by using a hash of the primary key. Sharding can dramatically improve performance by reducing the load on any single server, but it requires careful planning to avoid hotspots

72

and ensure that queries spanning multiple shards remain efficient.

- **Distributed SQL Databases:** Recent advances in database technology have given rise to distributed SQL databases that combine the benefits of traditional relational databases with horizontal scalability. Systems like Google Cloud Spanner or CockroachDB distribute data across many nodes while still providing SQL interfaces and strong consistency guarantees. These solutions are particularly attractive for SaaS applications that require both the transactional integrity of relational databases and the scalability of distributed systems.

Techniques for Efficient Query Execution

Scaling a database isn't only about the underlying hardware or distributed architecture—it's also about how queries are designed and executed. Consider the following best practices:

- **Optimizing Queries:** Even with a perfectly scaled database, inefficient queries can become bottlenecks. Use query analyzers and performance monitors to identify slow-running queries, and refactor them by adding appropriate indexes, avoiding expensive operations, and breaking complex queries into simpler ones when possible.

- **Using Connection Pools:** Database connection pools can manage a fixed number of connections to the database and reuse them for multiple queries. This avoids the overhead of establishing a new connection for every request and helps maintain predictable performance under load.

- **Read Replicas for Analytics:** For workloads that involve heavy analytics or reporting, it is often beneficial to route these queries to dedicated read replicas or even separate analytical databases. This separation ensures that real-time transactional performance remains unaffected by long-running analytical queries.

Handling High Concurrency and Transactional Loads

In a SaaS environment with many concurrent users, managing transactional loads efficiently is critical. This may involve adopting:

- **Optimistic and Pessimistic Concurrency Controls:** Depending on the expected collision rate of transactions, you might choose optimistic concurrency control (assuming conflicts are rare and handling them when they occur) or pessimistic locking (preventing conflicts by locking resources). Both approaches have trade-offs in terms of throughput and latency.

- **Batch Processing:** For write-heavy operations, consider batching updates to reduce the number of individual transactions. Batching can also be used for bulk inserts or updates, which can be scheduled during off-peak hours if real-time processing is not critical.

- **Asynchronous Processing:** Decoupling real-time transactional work from background processing can alleviate load. For example, logging, data aggregation, or post-transaction notifications might be handled asynchronously, reducing the time spent on critical transactional operations.

By combining vertical and horizontal scaling strategies, optimizing query performance, and managing concurrency wisely, SaaS providers can ensure that their databases continue to deliver high performance even as usage scales dramatically.

4.2 Data Partitioning and Sharding

As your SaaS application grows in size and complexity, a single monolithic database may struggle to provide the performance and reliability required. Data partitioning and sharding offer techniques to distribute data across multiple nodes, enabling your system to scale efficiently while maintaining fast query response times.

4.2.1 Horizontal vs. Vertical Partitioning

Partitioning can be broadly classified into two categories: horizontal and vertical partitioning. Both methods address performance challenges but differ in how data is divided.

Horizontal Partitioning

Horizontal partitioning (or sharding) involves dividing a table's rows into distinct groups, each stored on separate database nodes. This approach is particularly effective for SaaS applications because it allows different subsets of tenants or data ranges to be managed independently.

- **Benefits:** Horizontal partitioning can significantly reduce query response times by limiting the amount of data scanned during a query. It also improves write performance by spreading write operations across multiple nodes. In multi-tenant architectures, a common approach is to shard by tenant ID, ensuring that each tenant's data is stored on a separate shard, thereby minimizing contention.

- **Challenges:** Implementing horizontal partitioning requires careful planning to choose an effective sharding key. A poorly chosen sharding key may lead to "hot spots," where one shard handles disproportionate load, while others remain underutilized. Additionally, queries that span multiple shards can become complex and may require distributed query processing techniques.

Vertical Partitioning

Vertical partitioning involves dividing a table into multiple tables, each containing a subset of the columns. This method is useful when different columns have different usage patterns or when some columns are accessed far more frequently than others.

- **Benefits:** Vertical partitioning allows frequently accessed data to be stored separately from rarely used columns, reducing the data footprint for common queries and improving performance. It also simplifies caching strategies, as the "hot" columns can be managed independently.

- **Challenges:** Vertical partitioning can complicate data integrity and transactional consistency because the logical entity is split across multiple physical tables. Reconstructing the full record from separate partitions may require additional join operations, which could impact performance if not managed properly.

For many SaaS applications, a hybrid approach is often ideal. You might horizontally partition tenant data while using vertical partitioning to optimize individual table performance. The right combination depends on your data access patterns, query complexity, and the anticipated growth trajectory of your platform.

4.2.2 Managing Data Consistency

In distributed systems, managing data consistency becomes more challenging, particularly when data is partitioned or sharded across multiple nodes. SaaS applications often require strong consistency for transactional data while also needing to support eventual consistency for analytical or replicated data. Here are some key strategies:

Consistency Models

- **Strong Consistency:** In a strongly consistent system, all users see the same data at the same time. This model is often required for financial transactions, user authentication, and other critical operations. Achieving strong consistency typically requires synchronous replication and coordinated commit protocols, which can impact performance under high load.

- **Eventual Consistency:** In many cases, eventual consistency is acceptable and can dramatically improve scalability and performance. With eventual consistency, data changes propagate asynchronously across nodes. While there may be a brief window where different nodes have different versions of the data, the system eventually converges to a consistent state. This model is often used for non-critical data, analytics, or caching layers.

Distributed Transactions

When operations span multiple partitions or shards, ensuring consistency can require distributed transactions. Traditional two-phase commit (2PC) protocols provide strong consistency guarantees but introduce latency and complexity. Modern approaches include:

- **Saga Patterns:** A saga is a sequence of local transactions that update different partitions, each with a compensating transaction in case of failure. The saga pattern is well suited to SaaS environments where long-running transactions are acceptable if managed through eventual consistency.

- **Conflict Resolution Strategies:** In systems employing eventual consistency, conflict resolution strategies—such as last-write-wins or custom merge functions—can help reconcile divergent data states without the overhead of distributed locking.

Monitoring and Auditing Consistency

Ensuring data consistency in a multi-tenant SaaS system requires proactive monitoring:

- **Consistency Checks:** Regular audits and consistency checks can detect anomalies early. Automated tools can compare replicas or shards to identify discrepancies, triggering alerts if data drifts beyond acceptable limits.

- **Transaction Logging:** Detailed logging of transactional operations can help trace and resolve consistency issues when they occur. In addition, audit logs provide a historical record that is essential for troubleshooting and compliance audits.

By carefully selecting consistency models, implementing distributed transaction patterns where necessary, and actively monitoring for drift, SaaS providers can manage data consistency effectively—even in highly partitioned or sharded systems.

4.3 Caching Strategies

Caching is a critical element of data management for SaaS applications, offering significant performance improvements by reducing database load and accelerating data retrieval. However, effective caching strategies must balance performance gains with the complexity and cost of maintaining cache consistency. In this section, we delve into popular caching techniques, the use of in-memory data stores, and integration with content delivery networks (CDNs).

4.3.1 Redis, Memcached, and CDN Integration

In-Memory Data Stores

- **Redis:** Redis is a high-performance, in-memory key-value store that supports a variety of data structures, such as strings, hashes, lists, sets, and sorted sets. In SaaS applications, Redis is commonly used for caching session data, configuration settings, and frequently accessed query results. Its support for persistence, pub/sub messaging, and atomic operations makes it a versatile choice.

- For example, a SaaS platform might cache user permissions in Redis to minimize the load on the primary database and provide rapid authorization checks.

- **Memcached:** Memcached is another popular in-memory caching solution, valued for its simplicity and speed. It is ideal for storing small, frequently accessed data objects that do not require complex data structures or persistence. Although Memcached lacks some of Redis's advanced features, its lightweight nature and ease of deployment have made it a staple in many SaaS architectures.

Content Delivery Networks (CDNs)

- **Role of CDNs:** While in-memory caches like Redis and Memcached handle application-level data, CDNs focus on delivering static or cacheable content (such as images, stylesheets, and JavaScript files) quickly to users across the globe. A CDN caches content at edge locations, reducing latency and offloading traffic from origin servers.

  In a SaaS context, CDNs are essential for ensuring that user interfaces load rapidly, regardless of geographical location. They also contribute to improved reliability during peak usage periods.

- **Integration Best Practices:** Integrating a CDN involves setting proper cache control headers on your content, configuring invalidation policies to ensure that updates are reflected in a timely manner, and often combining CDN strategies with API caching for dynamic content. Advanced configurations may include using a CDN for caching API responses or even for serving personalized content with edge computing functions.

Layered Caching Architectures

For many SaaS platforms, an effective caching strategy involves multiple layers:

1. **Client-Side Caching:** Browsers and mobile applications can cache static assets and even certain API responses. This reduces network calls and speeds up the user experience.

2. **Application-Level Caching:** The application server can implement caching mechanisms (using in-memory stores like Redis) to hold frequently accessed data that might otherwise require database calls. This is particularly useful for data that does not change frequently or for computations that are expensive to perform repeatedly.

3. **Distributed Caching:** At the infrastructure level, distributed caching systems ensure that cache entries are shared among different application nodes, ensuring consistency and high availability. This can be crucial in multi-tenant environments where load is spread across many servers.

By combining these layers, you create a robust caching architecture that minimizes database load, accelerates response times, and scales effectively as your SaaS platform grows.

4.3.2 Trade-offs Between Performance and Cost

While caching can dramatically improve performance, it comes with its own set of trade-offs:

Cache Invalidation and Freshness

- **Stale Data vs. Performance:** One of the perennial challenges of caching is maintaining data freshness. Overly aggressive caching can lead to stale data, while frequent invalidation may negate the performance benefits. SaaS providers need to carefully design cache lifetimes and invalidation strategies that balance the need for speed with the need for accuracy.

- **Techniques for Cache Invalidation:** Common strategies include time-to-live (TTL) values, event-based invalidation (e.g., clearing cache entries when underlying data is updated), and versioning of cache keys. Implementing these techniques often requires tight integration between your database, application logic, and caching layer.

Cost Considerations

- **Operational Costs:** In-memory caches require dedicated hardware or cloud instances, which adds to operational costs. While services like Redis managed by cloud providers are highly available, they come at a premium compared to running open-source instances on self-managed infrastructure.
- **Scaling Cache Infrastructure:** As your SaaS platform scales, so does the cost of maintaining a large, distributed cache. Balancing the expense against the performance benefits is essential. Automated scaling of cache clusters, careful monitoring, and periodic reviews of cache hit ratios help optimize cost efficiency.

Complexity and Maintenance

- **Increased Architectural Complexity:** Integrating multiple caching layers, ensuring proper synchronization between them, and handling cache invalidation logic can increase the complexity of your application. Complexity can lead to harder-to-debug issues and may require additional development resources.
- **Monitoring and Analytics:** Establishing robust monitoring for your caching layer is essential. You need to track cache hit ratios, latency, and the frequency of cache invalidation events. This monitoring helps you fine-tune caching policies and anticipate scaling needs.

By analyzing the trade-offs between performance enhancements and associated costs, SaaS architects can design caching strategies that yield significant improvements in user experience while maintaining a cost-effective infrastructure.

Chapter 5: Security and Compliance in SaaS

Security and compliance are fundamental pillars for any successful SaaS application. As software moves from on-premises installations to a cloud-based, multi-tenant delivery model, the potential risks and regulatory requirements multiply. This chapter explores the challenges, strategies, and best practices in building a secure and compliant SaaS platform. We begin by examining authentication and authorization techniques, then transition to data privacy issues and regulatory compliance frameworks, and finally delve into secure development practices that help mitigate risks throughout the software lifecycle.

Throughout this chapter, we provide a comprehensive overview of:

- **Authentication and Authorization:** The systems, protocols, and design patterns that ensure only the right users gain access to the right resources.
- **Data Privacy and Compliance:** The regulatory environment affecting SaaS platforms—from GDPR to HIPAA—and the strategies to ensure data is protected both in transit and at rest.
- **Secure Development Practices:** How to embed security into every phase of development, from code reviews and

vulnerability assessments to secure API design and continuous monitoring.

In an era where data breaches and cyberattacks are increasingly common, and regulatory requirements evolve rapidly, understanding and implementing robust security and compliance measures is not optional—it's a competitive necessity.

5.1 Authentication and Authorization

Authentication and authorization are the twin pillars of access control in any SaaS solution. Authentication is the process of verifying a user's identity, while authorization determines what actions an authenticated user is permitted to perform. For SaaS applications—where the same application serves multiple organizations (tenants) with varied permissions—these processes must be both robust and flexible.

5.1.1 Overview of Authentication Mechanisms

Modern SaaS applications typically support multiple authentication mechanisms to accommodate a diverse user base. Here are some of the core methods:

Traditional Username and Password

For many years, the classic approach to authentication has been the use of a username and password. In a SaaS environment, this often includes:

- **Secure Storage of Credentials:** Passwords must be hashed and salted using modern cryptographic techniques (e.g., bcrypt, Argon2) before being stored in the database. This ensures that even if a breach occurs, the raw passwords remain undisclosed.

- **Multi-Factor Authentication (MFA):** MFA adds an extra layer of security by requiring users to provide additional proof of identity—such as a time-based one-time password (TOTP) from a mobile authenticator app or a hardware token—beyond just the password. This significantly reduces the risk of unauthorized access if passwords are compromised.

- **Account Lockout Policies:** To prevent brute-force attacks, SaaS applications often implement account lockout or throttling mechanisms. After a certain number of failed login attempts, the system temporarily disables the account or requires additional verification.

Federated Identity and Single Sign-On (SSO)

Many enterprises require the ability to integrate their existing identity providers (IdPs) into the SaaS platform. Federated identity protocols such as SAML (Security Assertion Markup Language), OAuth 2.0, and OpenID Connect (OIDC) allow users to authenticate using their organization's credentials. This approach offers several benefits:

- **Centralized Identity Management:** Organizations can manage user identities and policies centrally, reducing administrative overhead and ensuring consistency across multiple applications.

- **Improved User Experience:** Single Sign-On (SSO) allows users to log in once and access multiple systems without repeated authentication, thereby improving user convenience and reducing password fatigue.

- **Enhanced Security Posture:** By relying on enterprise-grade IdPs, SaaS platforms can inherit advanced security measures (such as adaptive authentication and risk-based policies) that might be too resource-intensive to implement independently.

Social and Third-Party Logins

For consumer-focused SaaS applications, offering social login options (using providers like Google, Facebook, or LinkedIn) can streamline the onboarding process. However, this method requires careful handling of third-party data and trust relationships. Key considerations include:

- **Data Sharing and Privacy:** Understand and document what user data is retrieved from social providers, and ensure that users are informed about how this data will be used.
- **Fallback Mechanisms:** Provide options for users to switch to traditional username/password authentication if they prefer not to use a social login.

Biometric and Adaptive Authentication

Emerging authentication technologies, such as biometrics (fingerprint, facial recognition) and adaptive authentication systems that evaluate risk factors (device fingerprinting, geolocation, behavior analysis), offer additional security benefits:

- **User Convenience:** Biometric authentication is both fast and secure, eliminating the need to remember complex passwords.
- **Contextual Security:** Adaptive systems adjust authentication requirements based on real-time risk assessment, such as requesting additional verification when login attempts are made from unusual locations or devices.

5.1.2 Authorization Strategies and Role-Based Access Control (RBAC)

Once a user's identity is confirmed, the next challenge is determining what that user is allowed to do. This is achieved through authorization mechanisms that enforce access controls at both the application and data levels.

Role-Based Access Control (RBAC)

RBAC is the most common method for managing permissions in SaaS applications. In an RBAC model, permissions are assigned to roles rather than directly to users. Users then inherit permissions based on their assigned roles. This approach offers several advantages:

- **Scalability:** By grouping permissions into roles, the system can efficiently manage access for a large number of users across multiple tenants.
- **Simplicity and Clarity:** RBAC provides clear, auditable policies that align with organizational hierarchies and job functions.
- **Flexibility:** Roles can be customized for different tenants, allowing for tailored access control based on each organization's needs.

Attribute-Based Access Control (ABAC)

For more granular control, many SaaS platforms adopt Attribute-Based Access Control (ABAC). Unlike RBAC, which is based solely on user roles, ABAC evaluates a combination of user attributes, resource characteristics, and environmental factors:

- **Contextual Decision Making:** ABAC can incorporate dynamic factors such as the time of access, location, or the sensitivity of the data being accessed. For example, a SaaS platform might restrict access to sensitive financial data if the request originates from an untrusted network.
- **Policy Flexibility:** ABAC policies can be fine-tuned to allow exceptions or enforce additional constraints, offering a more nuanced control mechanism for environments with complex security requirements.
- **Implementation Considerations:** ABAC systems are typically more complex to implement and manage compared

to RBAC, and they require robust auditing and monitoring to ensure policies are enforced correctly.

Decentralized and Fine-Grained Authorization

As SaaS platforms evolve to include microservices and API-driven architectures, authorization logic may become decentralized. In such cases, each microservice or API endpoint might enforce its own access controls, guided by a centralized policy engine or distributed token validation process. Key elements include:

- **Token-Based Authorization:** OAuth 2.0 and OIDC tokens often contain claims that specify user roles and permissions. These tokens are validated at each service endpoint to ensure that requests are authorized.
- **API Gateways:** API gateways can serve as a central point for enforcing security policies, including rate limiting, IP filtering, and content validation. They can inspect tokens, apply transformations, and route requests to backend services while maintaining consistent authorization logic.
- **Policy Engines:** Advanced systems may employ policy engines like Open Policy Agent (OPA) to dynamically evaluate authorization policies across multiple services. These engines allow policies to be updated centrally and distributed across the system, ensuring uniform enforcement.

5.1.3 Implementing Multi-Tenant Authorization

For SaaS platforms that support multiple tenants, the complexity of authorization increases significantly. It is imperative to ensure that a user from one tenant cannot access resources belonging to another tenant. Strategies for achieving this include:

- **Tenant Isolation in Access Control:** Each API call or query should include a tenant identifier, and the authorization layer should verify that the user's tenant matches the resource's

88

tenant. This check is fundamental to maintaining data privacy and security in a multi-tenant environment.

- **Scoped Tokens:** Tokens issued by the authentication service should include a scope or claim that denotes the tenant context. Services receiving the token can then validate that the tenant claim aligns with the resource being accessed.
- **Segregated User Interfaces:** On the client side, user interfaces should clearly segregate tenant data, reducing the risk of accidental cross-tenant exposure. For example, dashboards and management consoles should display tenant-specific data only after verifying the user's tenant affiliation.
- **Audit and Logging:** Comprehensive logging of all access attempts—including successful and failed authorization checks—is critical. Audit trails help identify potential breaches or misconfigurations and are essential for regulatory compliance.

By designing a robust authentication and authorization framework that incorporates multiple layers of security—from traditional passwords to adaptive and token-based methods—SaaS platforms can protect user data and prevent unauthorized access. In the following sections, we turn our attention to broader data protection measures and the regulatory environment that influences how SaaS providers secure and manage user data.

5.2 Data Privacy and Compliance

Data privacy and compliance are not merely technical challenges; they represent legal, ethical, and business imperatives. As SaaS providers collect, store, and process vast amounts of data across international boundaries, they must navigate an intricate web of regulations, standards, and best practices designed to protect user privacy. This section provides a deep dive into the core compliance frameworks, key regulatory requirements, and best practices for maintaining data privacy in a SaaS environment.

5.2.1 Regulatory Frameworks Impacting SaaS

SaaS providers often operate in a global environment where data privacy regulations vary widely between jurisdictions. Here are some of the most influential frameworks:

General Data Protection Regulation (GDPR)

The European Union's GDPR is one of the most comprehensive data protection regulations in the world. Key requirements include:

- **Data Subject Rights:** GDPR grants individuals rights such as access, rectification, and erasure (the "right to be forgotten"). SaaS applications must implement mechanisms that allow users to manage their data.
- **Consent and Transparency:** Organizations must obtain explicit consent before collecting and processing personal data. Privacy policies must be clear, concise, and easily accessible.
- **Data Protection Impact Assessments (DPIAs):** For high-risk processing activities, DPIAs are mandatory. These assessments help identify potential risks and define mitigation strategies.
- **Data Breach Notifications:** In the event of a data breach, organizations are required to notify regulatory authorities and affected users within a specified timeframe.
- **Cross-Border Data Transfers:** GDPR imposes strict rules on transferring personal data outside the European Economic Area (EEA), requiring adequate safeguards such as Standard Contractual Clauses or Binding Corporate Rules.

Health Insurance Portability and Accountability Act (HIPAA)

For SaaS platforms handling healthcare data in the United States, HIPAA sets stringent standards for protecting sensitive patient information. Key aspects include:

- **Privacy and Security Rules:** These rules define the standards for the use, disclosure, and safeguarding of protected health information (PHI).
- **Risk Analysis and Management:** Covered entities must conduct regular risk assessments to identify vulnerabilities and implement corrective measures.
- **Access Controls and Audit Trails:** HIPAA mandates strict access controls and comprehensive logging to ensure that PHI is only accessed by authorized personnel.
- **Business Associate Agreements (BAAs):** SaaS providers that handle PHI are considered business associates and must enter into BAAs with healthcare organizations, outlining responsibilities for data protection.

Payment Card Industry Data Security Standard (PCI DSS)

For SaaS applications that handle payment transactions, PCI DSS is critical:

- **Data Encryption:** Sensitive cardholder data must be encrypted during transmission and at rest.
- **Network Security:** Firewalls, intrusion detection systems, and regular security testing are required to safeguard payment data.
- **Access Control:** Strict policies and procedures must ensure that only authorized personnel can access payment information.
- **Regular Audits:** Compliance requires periodic audits by approved scanning vendors (ASVs) to ensure adherence to security standards.

Other Regulations and Standards

Depending on your target market, other regulations such as the California Consumer Privacy Act (CCPA), ISO/IEC 27001 (information security management), and industry-specific standards may apply. SaaS providers must keep abreast of evolving requirements and integrate them into their security and data governance policies.

5.2.2 Strategies for Ensuring Data Privacy

Given the diverse regulatory landscape, SaaS platforms must implement comprehensive strategies to protect data privacy:

Data Minimization and Purpose Limitation

- **Collect Only What You Need:** Adopt a data minimization strategy by only collecting data that is necessary for the functionality of the application. Unnecessary data collection increases risk and regulatory exposure.
- **Define Data Usage Purposes:** Clearly specify and document the purposes for which data is collected. This information must be communicated to users in clear terms and only used for those stated purposes.

Data Encryption and Secure Storage

- **Encryption at Rest and in Transit:** All sensitive data should be encrypted both when stored and during transmission. Use industry-standard encryption algorithms (e.g., AES-256) and secure transport protocols (e.g., TLS 1.2+).
- **Key Management:** Secure key management practices are critical. Keys should be stored separately from the encrypted data, with strict access controls and rotation policies in place.
- **Tokenization and Masking:** For especially sensitive data, consider tokenization or data masking techniques that replace sensitive values with non-sensitive placeholders.

Access Controls and Identity Management

- **Granular Access Policies:** Implement strict access control measures that ensure only authorized users can view or modify personal data. This includes both user-level access and administrative privileges.

- **Audit and Monitoring:** Continuous monitoring and detailed logging of data access and modifications are essential for detecting unauthorized activity and demonstrating compliance during audits.
- **Least Privilege Principle:** Adopt the principle of least privilege by granting users and systems the minimum level of access necessary to perform their functions.

Privacy by Design and Default

- **Incorporate Privacy into the Development Lifecycle:** Privacy by design means that data protection considerations are embedded into every stage of development—from initial design and architecture to deployment and maintenance.
- **Default Settings:** Ensure that the default configuration of the SaaS application is the most privacy-friendly option. Users should have to opt-in rather than opt-out of data sharing or tracking mechanisms.
- **Regular Privacy Impact Assessments (PIAs):** Conduct PIAs to evaluate how new features or changes to existing ones impact user privacy, and address any identified risks proactively.

5.2.3 Managing Data Breaches and Incident Response

No system is entirely immune to breaches. Effective incident response is vital to mitigating damage and maintaining user trust. Key components of a robust incident response strategy include:

Preparation and Prevention

- **Incident Response Plans:** Develop and document comprehensive incident response plans that outline roles, responsibilities, communication strategies, and escalation paths. These plans should be reviewed and updated regularly.

- **Regular Security Drills:** Conduct simulated breach scenarios and tabletop exercises to test the response plan and ensure that all team members know their roles during an incident.
- **Continuous Monitoring:** Implement real-time monitoring systems that can detect anomalies, suspicious activity, or unauthorized access. Tools for intrusion detection, network monitoring, and log analysis are essential in this regard.

Detection and Analysis

- **Automated Alerts:** Set up automated alerts for unusual behavior, such as spikes in failed login attempts, unauthorized data access, or unexpected system changes.
- **Forensic Analysis:** In the event of a breach, a forensic investigation must determine the scope and root cause. Detailed logs, audit trails, and system snapshots are critical for understanding the incident and preventing future occurrences.
- **Communication Protocols:** Clear communication channels should be established for notifying internal teams, affected users, and regulatory bodies if necessary. The timeliness and transparency of communication can be a deciding factor in regulatory compliance.

Containment, Eradication, and Recovery

- **Containment Strategies:** Rapidly isolate affected systems to prevent the breach from spreading. This might involve shutting down compromised components or revoking compromised credentials.
- **Eradication:** Once contained, remove malicious code, unauthorized access points, or vulnerabilities that allowed the breach to occur. Patch systems and update security policies as needed.

- **Recovery and Validation:** Restore affected systems from secure backups, validate that all threats have been removed, and closely monitor the system during the recovery phase.

Post-Incident Analysis and Improvement

- **Lessons Learned:** After the incident, conduct a thorough review of what went wrong and why. Document lessons learned and update security practices and response plans accordingly.
- **Regulatory Reporting:** Many regulations (such as GDPR) mandate reporting breaches to authorities within a strict timeframe. Ensure that your incident response process includes provisions for regulatory notifications and user communications.
- **User Compensation and Support:** In some cases, breaches may result in harm to users. A transparent, empathetic response—possibly including support services or compensation—can help rebuild trust.

By proactively addressing data privacy and compliance concerns and implementing robust incident response mechanisms, SaaS providers can reduce the impact of security incidents and comply with increasingly stringent regulatory requirements.

5.3 Secure Development Practices

Security must be an integral part of the software development lifecycle (SDLC) in a SaaS environment. Embedding security from the very beginning of the development process not only reduces vulnerabilities but also minimizes the long-term costs associated with patching and retrofitting solutions. In this section, we discuss best practices and methodologies that enable organizations to develop secure SaaS applications.

5.3.1 Secure Coding Standards

Secure coding standards are the foundation of any secure development process. These standards help prevent common vulnerabilities and ensure that developers follow consistent, best-practice guidelines. Key principles include:

Input Validation and Sanitization

- **Preventing Injection Attacks:** Validate and sanitize all user inputs to protect against SQL injection, cross-site scripting (XSS), and other injection attacks. Use parameterized queries and prepared statements to separate code from data.
- **White-Listing Over Black-Listing:** Employ white-listing approaches to ensure that only acceptable values are processed. This is particularly important for web applications that accept complex inputs.

Error Handling and Logging

- **Secure Error Reporting:** Avoid exposing sensitive information through error messages. Detailed error messages should be logged internally but not displayed to end users.
- **Log Security:** Ensure that logs do not contain sensitive data. Logs must be stored securely, with strict access controls to prevent unauthorized access.

Encryption and Cryptography

- **Strong Encryption Practices:** Use strong, industry-standard encryption algorithms for data at rest and in transit. Ensure that cryptographic keys are managed securely and rotated regularly.
- **Avoiding Deprecated Methods:** Regularly review cryptographic libraries and practices to avoid using outdated or insecure algorithms.

5.3.2 Secure API and Microservices Design

Modern SaaS applications often rely on APIs and microservices for functionality and scalability. Secure design in this domain involves:

API Security Best Practices

- **Authentication and Authorization for APIs:** APIs should implement robust authentication (using OAuth, JWT, or similar protocols) and verify that callers have the necessary permissions.
- **Rate Limiting and Throttling:** To prevent abuse, implement rate limiting on API endpoints. This protects against denial-of-service attacks and ensures fair usage across tenants.
- **Input and Output Validation:** Sanitize all inputs to APIs and validate outputs before sending them to clients.
- **API Gateway Integration:** Use an API gateway to centralize security controls, manage traffic, and enforce consistent security policies across all endpoints.

Secure Inter-Service Communication

- **Mutual TLS:** For communication between microservices, mutual TLS (mTLS) provides both authentication and encryption. This is critical for ensuring that only authorized services can communicate with each other.
- **Service Mesh Solutions:** Deploying a service mesh (such as Istio or Linkerd) can simplify secure inter-service communications by managing certificates, routing, and policy enforcement centrally.
- **Data Isolation in Microservices:** Each microservice should manage its own data and avoid exposing internal data structures. Secure interfaces and APIs ensure that data is accessed in a controlled manner.

5.3.3 Continuous Security Testing and DevSecOps

Security is not a one-time task—it requires continuous attention throughout the development lifecycle. DevSecOps integrates security practices into DevOps, enabling teams to build, test, and deploy secure code quickly.

Automated Code Analysis and Vulnerability Scanning

- **Static Application Security Testing (SAST):** Integrate SAST tools into your CI/CD pipeline to automatically scan code for vulnerabilities as it is written. These tools help identify common issues such as buffer overflows, insecure API usage, and code injection vulnerabilities.
- **Dynamic Application Security Testing (DAST):** Use DAST tools to simulate attacks on running applications, identifying vulnerabilities that only manifest at runtime.
- **Dependency Management:** Regularly update third-party libraries and monitor for known vulnerabilities using tools like Dependabot or Snyk. Ensure that external dependencies meet your security standards.

Penetration Testing and Security Audits

- **Regular Penetration Testing:** Schedule regular penetration tests—either internally or via third-party experts—to simulate real-world attacks and uncover hidden vulnerabilities.
- **Security Audits:** Conduct comprehensive audits of your code, configurations, and infrastructure to ensure adherence to security policies and best practices.

Secure CI/CD Pipelines

- **Pipeline Hardening:** Ensure that your CI/CD environment is secure. This includes restricting access, using signed code, and monitoring for unauthorized changes.
- **Secrets Management:** Integrate secret management tools into your CI/CD pipelines so that sensitive data (API keys, tokens, certificates) is never exposed in logs or code repositories.

- **Compliance Checks:** Incorporate compliance checks as part of your automated pipeline to ensure that deployments meet relevant security and regulatory standards.

5.3.4 Developer Training and a Security-First Culture

Technical measures alone are not enough to secure a SaaS platform—cultivating a security-first mindset across the organization is critical.

Security Awareness Training

- **Regular Training Sessions:** Provide ongoing training for developers, testers, and operations staff to keep them informed of the latest security threats and best practices.
- **Coding Best Practices:** Encourage adherence to secure coding guidelines, and ensure that developers understand the consequences of neglecting security measures.
- **Simulated Attack Scenarios:** Run regular "red team" exercises or simulated attack scenarios to help teams recognize vulnerabilities and respond effectively.

Cross-Department Collaboration

- **DevSecOps Integration:** Foster collaboration between development, operations, and security teams to ensure that security considerations are integrated into every phase of the SDLC.
- **Clear Accountability:** Establish clear roles and responsibilities for security within the organization. Everyone—from developers to executives—should understand their part in maintaining a secure environment.
- **Incident Response Drills:** Regularly test incident response plans with cross-functional teams to ensure that everyone is prepared in the event of a breach.

Chapter 6: SaaS Application Development

SaaS application development is the dynamic process of transforming innovative ideas into live, cloud-delivered products that serve multiple customers simultaneously. Unlike traditional software applications, a SaaS product must not only provide high-quality functionality but also be designed for rapid, iterative development and continuous delivery. In this chapter, we explore the essential building blocks of SaaS application development: backend frameworks and technologies, frontend frameworks for user interfaces, and the integration of continuous integration and deployment (CI/CD) practices that streamline development cycles.

Developing a SaaS product requires careful planning and strategic choices at every step—from selecting the appropriate programming languages and frameworks to architecting APIs that are both secure and scalable. In addition, the modern SaaS application must offer a seamless user experience on both the backend and frontend, and be supported by robust automation pipelines that enable fast, reliable releases. The remainder of this chapter is organized into three main sections:

1. **Backend Frameworks and Technologies** – We dive into the considerations for choosing a backend tech stack that supports

multi-tenant architectures, high performance, and rapid scalability. We also cover best practices for designing RESTful and other APIs that form the backbone of your application.

2. **Frontend Frameworks for SaaS** – This section explores the decision-making process behind choosing between single-page applications (SPAs) and multi-page applications (MPAs), and offers insights into popular frameworks like React, Angular, and Vue.js. We discuss how these choices impact user experience, performance, and long-term maintainability.

3. **Continuous Integration and Deployment (CI/CD)** – Finally, we explain the importance of automating the build, testing, and deployment process. We detail how CI/CD pipelines, feature flags, and canary releases help you iterate faster, reduce downtime, and ensure that your SaaS application remains stable as you continuously roll out new features.

Throughout this chapter, we emphasize that SaaS application development is as much an art as it is a science. It involves balancing trade-offs among speed, functionality, security, and user experience— all while operating in an environment where change is constant. By carefully considering the topics presented here, you will be well-prepared to tackle the unique challenges of SaaS development.

6.1 Backend Frameworks and Technologies

The backend of a SaaS application is responsible for business logic, data processing, and communication with databases, third-party services, and client interfaces. When developing the backend, you must choose a tech stack that supports scalability, performance, and maintainability while addressing the demands of a multi-tenant environment.

6.1.1 Choosing the Right Backend Tech Stack

Selecting a backend tech stack involves evaluating several key factors: the nature of your application, the expected load, the skill set of your development team, and the ease with which you can integrate third-party services. Below, we explore the core considerations when choosing your backend technology.

Language and Framework Considerations

- **Language Maturity and Community Support:** Popular languages such as Java, Python, JavaScript (Node.js), Ruby, and Go each have vibrant ecosystems. The maturity of these languages often correlates with the availability of well-maintained libraries and frameworks. For example, Java with Spring Boot, Python with Django or Flask, and Node.js with Express have been battle-tested in enterprise environments. Evaluate the community support, documentation, and long-term viability of the language and frameworks you choose.

- **Performance and Concurrency:** Some applications require handling thousands of concurrent connections or processing large volumes of data in real time. Languages like Go and Node.js are well-regarded for their efficient handling of concurrency. In contrast, frameworks in Java or Python might require additional optimizations or the use of asynchronous programming models (such as asyncio in Python or reactive programming in Java) to achieve similar performance levels.

- **Developer Productivity:** Rapid development is crucial for SaaS startups and evolving products. Frameworks that promote rapid prototyping, such as Ruby on Rails or Django, can reduce time-to-market. However, if your application demands extreme performance, you might consider more low-level or type-safe languages such as Go or even Java with its robust enterprise frameworks.

Architectural Patterns and Scalability

- **Monolithic vs. Microservices Approaches:** The choice between a monolithic architecture and microservices can greatly influence your tech stack. In a monolithic design, a single codebase handles all functionalities. This is often easier to develop initially but may become a bottleneck as the application scales. Microservices, on the other hand, decompose the application into smaller, independently deployable services. This modularity supports scalability and fault isolation but introduces complexity in terms of service communication and data consistency. Choose the pattern that aligns with your team's expertise and your product's growth trajectory.

- **RESTful APIs and Beyond:** Most SaaS applications expose their functionality through APIs. RESTful APIs remain the industry standard due to their simplicity and wide adoption. However, GraphQL is increasingly popular for applications that require flexible, efficient data retrieval. When designing your backend, consider whether your application benefits from the conventional structure of REST or if a more dynamic querying language like GraphQL would better serve your clients.

- **Event-Driven and Asynchronous Processing:** High-performance SaaS systems often need to handle tasks asynchronously. Message queues (such as RabbitMQ or Apache Kafka) can decouple processes and improve responsiveness. In this model, tasks such as sending emails, processing data, or updating analytics can be offloaded to background workers, ensuring that the main application remains responsive. Evaluating your application's workload will help you decide whether to adopt an event-driven architecture and which tools best fit your requirements.

Database and Persistence Strategies

- **Database Selection:** The choice of a database is integral to backend development. Relational databases (such as PostgreSQL, MySQL, or Microsoft SQL Server) are preferred for transactional applications with strong consistency requirements. NoSQL databases (like MongoDB, Cassandra, or DynamoDB) are often chosen for their ability to handle large volumes of unstructured data and for horizontal scaling. Hybrid approaches that combine both relational and NoSQL systems are also common, with different types of data stored in the system that best accommodates their usage patterns.

- **Object-Relational Mapping (ORM):** ORMs can simplify database interactions by mapping database tables to language-specific objects. Frameworks like Hibernate (Java), SQLAlchemy (Python), or Sequelize (Node.js) reduce the need to write boilerplate SQL code and allow developers to interact with the database using familiar language constructs. However, be cautious of performance implications; sometimes direct SQL queries are necessary for complex or high-performance operations.

- **Multi-Tenancy Data Models:** In SaaS, the database must support multi-tenancy. This involves strategies such as shared schemas with tenant identifiers, separate schemas, or isolated databases per tenant. Your backend technology should allow you to implement these models without compromising performance or security.

Scalability and Fault Tolerance

- **Horizontal Scaling:** Choose frameworks that support stateless processing, making it easier to scale horizontally. A stateless backend ensures that new instances can be added or removed without affecting the overall state of the application. This

104

design principle is essential for cloud environments where auto-scaling is common.

- **Caching Mechanisms:** Integrate caching at multiple levels within your backend. In-memory caching systems like Redis or Memcached can accelerate data retrieval, while application-level caching reduces the load on the database. Caching should be carefully designed to maintain consistency and ensure that stale data does not compromise the user experience.

- **Resilience and Recovery:** Build fault tolerance into your backend by employing techniques such as circuit breakers, retries, and graceful degradation. Libraries and frameworks often provide built-in support for these patterns, helping to mitigate the impact of service failures and ensure that the system continues to function under adverse conditions.

Microservices and Containerization

- **Containerization with Docker:** Containerization has revolutionized how backends are developed and deployed. Docker provides an isolated, reproducible environment that simplifies dependency management and scaling. When combined with orchestration tools like Kubernetes, containerization allows for rapid, reliable deployment of microservices.

- **Service Communication:** In a microservices architecture, inter-service communication is key. Consider using lightweight protocols such as gRPC for high-performance communication or leveraging RESTful APIs where simplicity is desired. Effective service discovery and load balancing are also critical components in a containerized environment.

By evaluating these aspects and choosing a backend tech stack that aligns with your application's requirements, you can build a resilient foundation that supports rapid development and scalable performance.

6.1.2 API Design Best Practices

APIs are the lifeblood of modern SaaS applications, serving as the bridge between the backend and various clients—including web, mobile, and third-party integrations. A well-designed API not only simplifies development but also ensures security, scalability, and a seamless user experience.

RESTful API Design

- **Resource-Oriented Design:** RESTful APIs are built around the concept of resources. Each resource (e.g., users, orders, products) should have a unique URL and support standard HTTP methods (GET, POST, PUT/PATCH, DELETE). A clear, consistent URL structure and proper use of HTTP status codes are critical for intuitive API design.

- **Statelessness:** RESTful APIs are inherently stateless, meaning that each request contains all the information necessary to process it. This simplifies scalability and fault tolerance since each server can handle any request without relying on previous interactions.

- **Versioning:** As your API evolves, you must manage changes without breaking existing client implementations. Versioning strategies—such as including a version number in the URL (e.g., /v1/users) or using request headers—help maintain backward compatibility while allowing for iterative improvements.

- **Documentation:** Comprehensive documentation is crucial for API adoption. Tools like Swagger/OpenAPI enable you to create interactive documentation that both developers and third parties can use to understand and test your API endpoints.

GraphQL and Alternative Paradigms

- **Flexible Data Queries:** GraphQL offers an alternative to REST by allowing clients to request only the data they need. This flexibility can reduce over-fetching and under-fetching issues common in RESTful APIs.

- **Single Endpoint:** Instead of multiple resource-specific endpoints, GraphQL uses a single endpoint to handle all queries and mutations. This simplifies client development but requires robust query validation and rate limiting.

- **Schema-Driven Development:** GraphQL requires a well-defined schema that describes the data types, queries, and mutations available. This schema acts as a contract between the backend and clients, promoting consistency and clarity.

Security and Rate Limiting

- **Token-Based Authentication:** Protect your API endpoints with token-based authentication (e.g., OAuth 2.0, JWT). Tokens should encapsulate the user's identity and permissions, and be verified on each request.

- **Rate Limiting and Throttling:** Implement rate limiting to prevent abuse and ensure fair use among tenants. Rate limiting not only protects against denial-of-service attacks but also stabilizes the performance of your API during peak load times.

- **Input Validation:** Validate all incoming data to protect against injection attacks and ensure that only well-formed data reaches your business logic. This is especially important in public APIs where user inputs can be unpredictable.

Error Handling and Monitoring

- **Meaningful Error Responses:** Design error messages that are informative for developers yet do not expose sensitive information. Consistent error structures, including error codes and messages, make it easier to diagnose issues.

- **Logging and Monitoring:** Integrate robust logging to capture API usage patterns, errors, and performance metrics. Monitoring tools can alert you to unusual activity, enabling rapid response to issues as they arise.

By adhering to these best practices, your API will be secure, efficient, and easy to integrate, forming a solid foundation for your SaaS application's functionality.

6.2 Frontend Frameworks for SaaS

While the backend ensures data processing and business logic, the frontend is the interface through which users interact with your SaaS application. A robust frontend framework is essential for delivering a responsive, intuitive, and engaging user experience. In this section, we explore the considerations behind choosing between single-page applications (SPAs) and multi-page applications (MPAs) and review popular frameworks such as React, Angular, and Vue.js.

6.2.1 SPA vs. MPA in SaaS Applications

Deciding between a Single-Page Application (SPA) and a Multi-Page Application (MPA) is one of the first choices a SaaS developer must make. Both approaches have their merits, and the decision largely depends on the desired user experience, performance requirements, and development complexity.

Single-Page Applications (SPAs)

- **Seamless User Experience:** SPAs load a single HTML page and dynamically update content as users interact with the application. This approach minimizes page reloads, leading to a smoother, more fluid user experience. SPAs are particularly well-suited for applications that require high interactivity and real-time updates.

- **Client-Side Rendering:** In SPAs, most of the rendering occurs on the client side using JavaScript frameworks. This can reduce the load on the server and enable complex client-side logic.

- **Challenges with SPAs:** Despite their advantages, SPAs can present challenges such as initial load time, search engine optimization (SEO) difficulties, and increased client-side complexity. Developers often mitigate these issues with techniques like code-splitting, lazy loading, and server-side rendering (SSR) for critical pages.

Multi-Page Applications (MPAs)

- **Traditional Navigation:** MPAs consist of multiple HTML pages, each loaded separately. This approach is more traditional and may be easier to implement for content-heavy sites where SEO is a priority.

- **Server-Side Rendering:** MPAs typically rely on server-side rendering, ensuring that each page is fully rendered before being sent to the client. This can enhance initial load performance and improve SEO.

- **When to Choose MPAs:** MPAs are often a good choice for SaaS applications that do not require highly dynamic interfaces or where search engine discoverability is critical. However, they can be less fluid than SPAs when it comes to user interactions and require more full-page refreshes.

Hybrid Approaches

- **Progressive Web Apps (PWAs):** Many modern SaaS applications blend SPA and MPA techniques using Progressive Web App principles. PWAs offer offline support, push notifications, and app-like experiences while retaining the SEO benefits of server-side rendering.

- **Isomorphic Applications:** In an isomorphic (or universal) application, the same code runs on both the client and server, allowing for initial server-side rendering followed by client-side interactivity. This approach can provide the best of both worlds—fast load times, SEO benefits, and dynamic user interactions.

By understanding the trade-offs between SPAs and MPAs, you can choose a frontend architecture that best suits your SaaS application's functional and performance requirements.

6.2.2 Using React, Angular, or Vue.js

Once you've decided on the overall approach, the next step is to select a frontend framework. Today, the most popular frameworks—React, Angular, and Vue.js—each offer unique benefits. Here, we compare them in the context of SaaS application development.

React

- **Component-Based Architecture:** React's component-based model allows developers to build encapsulated, reusable UI components. This modularity simplifies maintenance and accelerates development cycles.

- **Virtual DOM for Performance:** React uses a virtual DOM to minimize direct manipulations of the real DOM, resulting in faster updates and improved performance in dynamic applications.

- **Ecosystem and Flexibility:** React's ecosystem includes a vast array of third-party libraries, state management tools (such as Redux or MobX), and routing solutions (like React Router). This flexibility makes React a strong choice for complex, interactive SaaS platforms.

- **Learning Curve:** Although React itself is relatively simple, the surrounding ecosystem can be daunting for new developers. However, once mastered, React's flexibility and performance benefits often outweigh the initial learning curve.

Angular

- **Comprehensive Framework:** Angular is a full-fledged framework that provides an all-in-one solution for building web applications. It includes built-in support for routing, form validation, dependency injection, and more. This integrated approach can simplify development by reducing the need for third-party libraries.

- **TypeScript-Based:** Angular is built using TypeScript, a statically typed superset of JavaScript. This offers advantages in terms of code reliability, maintainability, and better tooling with features like autocompletion and type checking.

- **Structured Development:** Angular's opinionated architecture and modular structure can help enforce coding best practices and consistency across large teams, making it a solid choice for enterprise-level SaaS applications.

- **Steeper Learning Curve:** Because Angular is a complete framework with many built-in features, it has a steeper learning curve. However, for teams that appreciate structure and a comprehensive feature set, Angular can greatly accelerate development once mastered.

Vue.js

- **Progressive Framework:** Vue.js is designed to be incrementally adoptable. It can be integrated into existing projects without a full rewrite and scaled up to build complex single-page applications.

- **Simplicity and Ease of Learning:** Vue's syntax is simple and well-documented, making it accessible for developers new to frontend frameworks. Its gentle learning curve is often cited as a major advantage.

- **Flexible Integration:** Vue can function as a view layer for an existing backend or be used to develop a full-fledged single-page application. This flexibility makes it an attractive option for startups and smaller teams that require rapid development.

- **Community and Ecosystem:** Although Vue's ecosystem is not as extensive as React's or Angular's, it is rapidly growing, with mature state management solutions (Vuex) and routing libraries (Vue Router) available for complex applications.

Each of these frameworks has its strengths and is well-suited for different types of SaaS applications. When selecting a framework, consider the complexity of your user interface, the expertise of your development team, and the long-term maintainability of the codebase.

6.3 Continuous Integration and Deployment (CI/CD)

Rapid iteration and frequent releases are key advantages of SaaS development, and a well-architected CI/CD pipeline is essential for delivering new features and bug fixes reliably and safely. In this section, we explore the principles and practices of continuous integration, continuous deployment, and techniques like feature flags and canary releases that help maintain service quality while pushing code to production quickly.

6.3.1 CI/CD Pipeline Automation

Fundamentals of CI/CD

- **Continuous Integration (CI):** CI is the practice of merging all developer working copies to a shared repository several times a day. Automated build and test processes run on each merge, ensuring that new code integrates smoothly and that any errors are caught early in the development cycle.

- **Continuous Deployment (CD):** CD extends CI by automatically deploying code changes to production as soon as they pass all testing stages. This minimizes the time between code being written and it being available to users, enabling rapid feedback and iterative improvement.

Implementing a CI/CD Pipeline

- **Version Control Integration:** Your pipeline begins with a version control system (e.g., Git) where all code is stored. Every change is tracked, and branch management strategies (such as GitFlow or trunk-based development) are adopted to maintain code quality.

- **Automated Testing:** An effective pipeline integrates various testing stages—unit tests, integration tests, and end-to-end tests. Automated tests catch errors early and ensure that new code does not break existing functionality.

- **Build Automation:** Tools such as Jenkins, GitLab CI, CircleCI, or GitHub Actions can be configured to automatically build your application upon code changes. Build automation ensures consistency and reduces the risk of manual errors.

- **Deployment Automation:** Deployment scripts, container orchestration, and infrastructure-as-code tools are integrated into the CI/CD pipeline. These ensure that the deployment process is repeatable, versioned, and can be rolled back in case of issues.

Monitoring and Feedback Loops

- **Continuous Monitoring:** Integrate monitoring tools to track application performance, error rates, and resource usage after each deployment. Automated alerts and dashboards help teams quickly detect and respond to anomalies.

- **Feedback Integration:** Feedback loops from production monitoring, user analytics, and error logging are fed back into the development process. This allows for continuous refinement of the codebase and the CI/CD pipeline itself.

6.3.2 Feature Flags and Canary Releases

As you move toward continuous deployment, you need mechanisms to mitigate risks associated with pushing new features to production. Two critical techniques are feature flags and canary releases.

Feature Flags

- **Dynamic Feature Management:** Feature flags (also known as feature toggles) allow you to enable or disable specific functionalities without deploying new code. This provides a way to test new features with a subset of users before rolling them out globally.

- **Safe Rollouts:** With feature flags, you can deploy code that contains new features but keep them disabled until you are confident in their stability. This technique reduces the risk of introducing bugs that affect the entire user base.

- **Granular Control:** Feature flags can be used for A/B testing, allowing you to gather user feedback and performance data for new features. They also facilitate rapid rollback if issues are detected, as you can simply disable the flag to remove the feature from production.

- **Implementation Considerations:** Ensure that feature flags are integrated into your CI/CD process and that their state is managed in a secure, versioned manner. Over time, legacy flags should be cleaned up to reduce complexity.

Canary Releases

- **Incremental Deployments:** A canary release strategy involves rolling out new changes to a small percentage of production servers or users initially. By exposing only a fraction of your user base to the new release, you can monitor for issues without impacting everyone.

- **Real-World Testing:** Canary releases provide a controlled environment to test how new features perform under actual load conditions. Metrics such as error rates, latency, and user engagement are closely monitored during the canary phase.

- **Rollout Automation:** CI/CD tools can be configured to gradually increase the percentage of traffic directed to the new version based on performance benchmarks. If problems are detected, traffic can be immediately reverted to the previous stable version.

- **Integration with Load Balancers:** Load balancers and API gateways can be configured to support canary releases by routing a small fraction of requests to the new version. This enables seamless switching between versions with minimal disruption.

Ensuring Rollback and Recovery

- **Automated Rollback Mechanisms:** In the event that a new release fails to meet performance or stability standards, automated rollback mechanisms ensure that the system can revert to a known good state. This is crucial in maintaining high availability and a positive user experience.

- **Testing Rollback Procedures:** Regularly test your rollback procedures as part of your CI/CD process. Knowing that you can quickly recover from a failed release is a vital aspect of risk management in SaaS development.

Chapter 7: Performance Optimization and Monitoring

A central hallmark of high-quality SaaS platforms is consistent, reliable performance under rapidly changing workloads. Customers expect near-instantaneous interactions, whether they are performing routine tasks or running complex data processes. At the same time, your application must operate smoothly across a broad spectrum of tenants—ranging from small teams to global enterprises—each placing unique and sometimes unpredictable demands on your system. To live up to such expectations, you must not only optimize every aspect of your service stack for performance but also maintain robust monitoring practices so that issues can be detected and corrected before they escalate into user-facing outages.

In this chapter, we examine the end-to-end journey of **performance optimization** and the instrumentation, logging, and analytics that support it. We begin by defining the key performance metrics that illuminate your service's operational health. We then delve into **application performance optimization**, addressing everything from low-level code efficiencies to sophisticated caching layers. Following that, we explore **observability**—the discipline of collecting logs, metrics, and traces that reveal how your system behaves in real time.

Finally, we discuss advanced strategies for capacity planning and adopting a continuous improvement mindset that ensures your SaaS offering keeps pace with evolving user demands.

Collectively, these practices enable you to move beyond reactive firefighting and adopt a proactive stance toward performance, anticipating issues before they affect end users. By weaving robust monitoring and optimization into your development lifecycle, you equip your SaaS product with the resilience, adaptability, and user satisfaction needed to thrive in highly competitive markets.

7.1 Performance Metrics for SaaS

A robust performance optimization strategy begins by defining **what** to measure and **why** it matters. Without clear metrics, teams struggle to decide where to invest resources or how to evaluate the impact of changes. In this section, we identify the key performance indicators (KPIs) and how to gather actionable insights through specialized tools and platforms that track them. The focus is on the technical vantage point: how well your application handles concurrent loads, responds to requests, and uses underlying infrastructure resources.

7.1.1 Defining Key Performance Indicators (KPIs)

Why KPIs Matter

KPIs are numerical representations of your system's operational health and user experience. They map the raw data from your application or infrastructure to concepts of reliability, scalability, and efficiency. In a SaaS context, where multiple customers share the same underlying resources, well-designed KPIs enable you to spot emergent performance issues, attribute them to specific root causes, and prioritize improvements based on their impact on tenant satisfaction.

Example scenario:

- A sudden increase in average API latency might indicate that your load balancing strategy is not distributing traffic effectively. Alternatively, it could signal a surge in database writes from a new tenant pushing large data batches. By correlating latency metrics with resource usage and request logs, you can quickly identify the culprit.

Categories of KPIs

1. **User-Centric Metrics**

   - **Response Time (Latency):** How long a request or operation takes from the user's perspective. Shorter response times generally mean higher satisfaction. This metric often subdivides into the 95th or 99th percentile for deeper granularity.
   - **Error Rate:** The percentage of requests resulting in errors—whether HTTP status codes in the 4xx/5xx range or application-specific error codes. Spikes in error rates can pinpoint code regressions or resource contention.
   - **Time to First Byte (TTFB):** Specifically measures the time from the moment a user's request leaves the client until the first byte of the response is received. TTFB can reveal networking or server-side bottlenecks.
   - **Apdex Score:** A user satisfaction index derived from specified response thresholds. It effectively translates response times into a single measure of user experience.

2. **System Health Metrics**

   - **CPU Utilization:** Tracks the percentage of CPU time consumed by your application. Persistent high utilization may indicate a need for code optimization or additional compute resources.

- **Memory Usage and Garbage Collection:** Monitors the portion of RAM in use, memory leaks, or inefficiencies in memory allocation. For garbage-collected languages, analyzing GC pause times can be critical to maintain smooth performance.
- **I/O Throughput:** Measures how quickly your system can read from or write to disk, network, or external services. Low throughput or high I/O wait times often lead to queue backlogs.
- **Queue Depth:** In systems using asynchronous messaging or background job queues, queue length reveals how quickly tasks are being consumed vs. produced. A consistently growing queue indicates a processing bottleneck.

3. **Scalability Metrics**

- **Requests per Second (RPS) or Transactions per Second (TPS):** A direct measure of throughput. If your SaaS handles more requests than it did a month ago, does performance remain stable?
- **Resource Saturation:** Often expressed as load averages, concurrency levels, or thread usage. Knowing how close the system is to saturation thresholds helps plan for capacity expansions.
- **Database Query Load:** Tracking the read/write ratio, average query execution time, or query concurrency provides insight into how well the data layer scales under load.

4. **Business-Related Technical Metrics**

- **Tenant-Specific Resource Consumption:** In a multi-tenant environment, large customers might dominate usage. Monitoring tenant-level breakdowns ensures no single client starves others.

- ○ **Cost Efficiency and Infrastructure Spend:** Evaluating how resource usage correlates with your monthly cloud bill can steer optimizations that reduce cost without compromising performance.
- ○ **User Adoption Patterns:** While not purely a technical metric, usage growth can foresee future performance demands. A sudden wave of new sign-ups might require proactive scaling.

7.1.2 Tools and Platforms for Monitoring

Essential Requirements

Before diving into specific products, we should outline the features that any robust monitoring tool or platform should offer:

- **Real-Time Metrics and Historical Trends:** The ability to see second-by-second or minute-by-minute data, along with aggregated historical views.
- **Scalability:** A monitoring platform that can handle the ingestion of large volumes of metrics and logs without itself becoming a bottleneck.
- **Configurable Alerting:** Mechanisms to set threshold-based or anomaly detection alerts, ensuring teams know immediately about potential performance degradations.
- **Integration with Other Tools:** The ability to correlate metrics with logs, traces, or other data sources for holistic observability.

Commonly Used Monitoring Solutions

1. **Prometheus and Grafana Stack**

   - ○ **Prometheus** pulls metrics from instrumented applications and stores them as time-series data. It is known for its custom query language (PromQL) and easy integration.

- **Grafana** visualizes the data from Prometheus (or other sources) in dashboards. Engineers can slice and dice metrics, set up alerts, and overlay multiple data sources.

- **Pros/Cons:** The open-source nature and robust community make it a popular choice. However, large-scale usage demands careful architecture of Prometheus servers and storage.

2. **Commercial APM (Application Performance Monitoring) Tools**

- **New Relic, Datadog, Dynatrace, AppDynamics**: These solutions collect metrics, logs, and traces, providing deep insights into code-level performance and user transactions.

- **Advantages:** Offers out-of-the-box instrumentation, advanced analytics, and (in many cases) AI-driven anomaly detection.

- **Potential Limitations:** Licensing can be expensive, and certain specialized features might require additional modules or usage fees.

3. **SaaS Monitoring Services**

- Some developers prefer managed monitoring products from cloud vendors (e.g., AWS CloudWatch, Azure Monitor, Google Cloud Monitoring).

- They integrate tightly with other cloud services but might offer fewer customization options or less synergy if your SaaS is multi-cloud.

4. **OpenTelemetry Ecosystem**

- OpenTelemetry is an open standard for instrumenting, generating, and exporting telemetry data (metrics, logs, traces).
- Gaining traction as a universal approach that decouples data collection from specific platforms.
- Ideal for multi-language, polyglot environments seeking consistent instrumentation.

Setting Up a Monitoring Pipeline

A typical pipeline might look like this:

1. **Instrumentation:** Embed libraries or SDKs in your code to capture low-level metrics (latency, CPU usage, function timings).
2. **Data Collection:** Use an agent or direct exports to push or pull metrics from each service or container.
3. **Central Storage:** Store these time-series metrics in a scalable backend (Prometheus, InfluxDB, or a commercial APM's data store).
4. **Analysis and Visualization:** Use dashboards to display real-time metrics and historical trends.
5. **Alerts and Notifications:** Configure threshold-based or anomaly-based alerts. Alerts might connect to Slack, PagerDuty, or email distribution lists.
6. **Feedback Loop:** Observations from monitoring lead to iterative improvements in code, configuration, or infrastructure sizing. Over time, performance issues become less frequent and easier to resolve.

Ensuring your monitoring solution covers the entire stack (front-end, back-end, and infrastructure) fosters end-to-end visibility, making it simpler to pinpoint precisely where performance bottlenecks appear.

7.2 Application Performance Optimization

With performance metrics established and monitoring in place, your next priority is to **optimize** each layer of the SaaS application—improving speed, reducing latency, and stabilizing throughput under load. This section covers an array of techniques and methodologies aimed at wringing maximum efficiency from your code, data storage, and network pathways. A well-optimized application not only ensures a better user experience but can also significantly cut infrastructure costs.

7.2.1 Code-Level and Algorithmic Optimization

Profiling and Benchmarking

- **Identifying Bottlenecks:** Tools such as profilers (e.g., VisualVM for JVM languages, pprof for Go, Perf for Linux, or language-specific ones) provide in-depth visibility into which functions consume the most CPU time or memory allocations. Even small "hot spots" in your code can quickly balloon into major slowdowns under concurrent loads.
- **Micro-Benchmarking:** In addition to high-level profiling, micro-benchmarks can measure the cost of specific routines. By methodically testing function call overhead, loop performance, or library usage, you gain the clarity to optimize your code at a granular level.
- **Continuous Assessment:** Incorporate profiling into your continuous integration setup. By automatically running performance tests after each new feature, you can detect regressions early.

Algorithmic Complexity

- **Choosing Efficient Data Structures:** Using an $O(n)$ data structure where an $O(\log n)$ or $O(1)$ alternative exists can lead to substantial performance improvements, especially under concurrency. For instance, if you rely heavily on searching or sorting, consider balanced trees, tries, or specialized indexes.

- **Batch Processing vs. Item-by-Item:** Instead of processing each transaction individually, batch them to reduce overhead—particularly relevant if your SaaS handles large volumes of small tasks.
- **Asynchronous and Non-Blocking Patterns:** Move from blocking I/O to asynchronous or reactive programming when feasible, so that threads aren't idly blocked waiting for external calls. This shift can significantly improve concurrency and reduce required compute resources.

Language-Specific Techniques

Every programming language or framework has its unique set of performance considerations. For example:

- **Java / JVM:** Tuning garbage collection parameters (like the G1 GC or ZGC) can reduce pause times and maintain throughput. Using ephemeral objects sparingly can also reduce GC overhead.
- **Node.js / JavaScript:** Avoid synchronous file I/O in the main event loop. Use streams and consider thread pooling for CPU-intensive tasks via worker threads.
- **Python:** Leverage native code extensions (NumPy) or concurrency primitives (asyncio) where possible. For truly CPU-bound tasks, consider multi-process or compiled modules in C.
- **Go:** Because Go uses goroutines and a concurrency-friendly runtime, optimizing includes controlling goroutine sprawl, managing channel usage, and watching for memory leaks in slices or maps.

7.2.2 Database and Query Optimization

Your database layer is often the heart of a SaaS application—storing critical tenant data, user information, and system logs. Even if your application code is well-tuned, suboptimal database schemas or queries can degrade performance quickly.

Schema Design and Indexing

- **Normalization vs. Denormalization:** Striking a balance is crucial. Overly normalized schemas can lead to excessive joins, whereas excessive denormalization can lead to duplicated data that complicates updates. Evaluate query patterns to decide the right approach.
- **Index Strategies:** For frequently queried columns, add indexes—but be careful not to over-index. Each index adds overhead for write operations. Consider composite indexes if queries filter by multiple columns.
- **Covering Indexes:** In some relational databases, a covering index (one that includes all columns used by a query) can eliminate the need to read the table data, drastically speeding up reads.
- **Partitioning:** For large tables, partitioning by date ranges, tenant IDs, or other categories can reduce index size and speed queries by scanning only the relevant partition.

Optimizing SQL Queries

- **Explain Plans:** Most relational database management systems offer "EXPLAIN" or similar functionality to illustrate how queries run. By studying these query plans, you can identify table scans, suboptimal joins, or other inefficiencies.
- **Parameterization and Prepared Statements:** Parameterized queries help caching at the database level and prevent repeated parsing of similar SQL statements. This often reduces overhead and can mitigate injection risks.
- **Join Strategies:** Minimizing the number of large joins can drastically reduce query execution times. Alternatively, if your

queries consistently join the same tables, consider merging or using materialized views if that suits your data flow.

Caching Approaches

- **In-Memory Caches:** Tools like Redis or Memcached can hold frequently accessed data. By retrieving data from cache instead of the database, you reduce query load and decrease response latency.
- **Database Caches:** Many databases have built-in caching (e.g., MySQL's query cache). Tuning these caches for your workloads can yield performance benefits, though it also imposes overhead for invalidations.
- **Application-Level Caches:** At the application tier, selectively caching certain computations or aggregated results can expedite repeated requests. Just be mindful of eviction policies and stale data.

7.2.3 Web Performance Tuning (Frontend and API Layers)

Although the backend often receives the most attention for performance improvements, end users typically measure speed in terms of **how quickly pages load** and **how responsive the interface feels**. Here, we focus on the front-end aspects of SaaS performance, as well as the design of your API endpoints.

Front-End Optimization

- **Asset Minification and Compression:** Minify JavaScript, CSS, and HTML to reduce file sizes. Leverage Brotli or Gzip compression so that these files travel over the network in a compressed form.
- **Bundling and Code Splitting:** Large front-end codebases can be split into smaller chunks, which load on demand. This approach reduces initial page load time, especially helpful if your SaaS application has rarely used modules.

- **Lazy Loading:** Defer loading images and other heavy assets until the user scrolls them into view or requests them explicitly. This can drastically shorten the time-to-interactive for content above the fold.
- **Browser Caching Headers:** Setting appropriate cache-control headers (max-age, ETag, or last-modified) helps browsers avoid re-downloading unchanged static assets.
- **DOM and Rendering Bottlenecks:** Overly complex DOM trees or frequent reflows can degrade client-side performance. Tools like Lighthouse (in Chrome) or WebPageTest help diagnose layout thrashing, large painting tasks, or JS main-thread contention.

API Endpoint Efficiency

- **Pagination and Limiting:** Return only the data each client needs—use pagination for large result sets, partial responses (fields filtering), or segment data retrieval to avoid "kitchen sink" endpoints.
- **Statelessness and Caching:** In RESTful designs, ensure GET requests for static or infrequently changing data set cache-friendly headers. For GraphQL-based APIs, consider query caching, though it can be more complex due to dynamic queries.
- **Bulk Operations vs. Chatty Requests:** Instead of multiple small requests, clients can batch operations if the server supports it. Conversely, if your API encourages extremely large payloads, ensure the system can handle chunking or streaming without blocking.
- **Rate-Limit Handling:** If your SaaS throttles calls to protect infrastructure, design endpoints and clients to handle 429 Too Many Requests or similar responses gracefully, with backoff strategies.

7.2.4 Infrastructure and Network Optimization

Even the best-optimized code and database queries run atop some infrastructure stack—servers, containers, or cloud-based VMs. Network paths, container orchestration, load balancing, and storage tiers each add potential latencies or overheads.

Load Balancing and Horizontal Scaling

- **Load Balancer Configuration:** A well-tuned load balancer (e.g., Nginx, HAProxy, AWS ALB/ELB) should distribute traffic uniformly while providing health checks. You can route traffic by session or round-robin, but if certain endpoints require high concurrency, you may apply special rules.
- **Autoscaling Policies:** Cloud services often provide auto-scaling based on CPU, memory, or custom metrics. Setting the right thresholds ensures that your SaaS can handle traffic spikes without overprovisioning.
- **Session Stickiness:** If your application demands stateful sessions, you might need session stickiness. However, for maximum concurrency, design your system to be stateless at the application tier, so requests can go to any server instance.

Container and Orchestration Considerations

- **Efficient Resource Allocations:** Container-based deployments require specifying CPU and memory requests and limits. Overly generous allocations waste resources; overly tight ones lead to throttling or OOM (out of memory) kills, harming performance.
- **Node-Level Optimization:** Certain kernels or operating systems might require tuning of network buffers, file descriptor limits, or TCP keepalive intervals for high concurrency.
- **Rolling Updates:** Orchestrators like Kubernetes can roll out new application versions gradually. Ensuring minimal downtime and consistent performance during these updates fosters a better user experience.

Network and CDN Usage

- **Content Delivery Networks (CDNs):** Serving static assets, images, or even partial dynamic data from edge nodes reduces latency for globally distributed users. Integrating a CDN can offload a large portion of traffic from your origin servers.
- **HTTP/2 and TLS Handshakes:** HTTP/2 supports multiplexing, reducing overhead for multiple simultaneous requests. Ensuring your TLS handshake overhead is optimized—possibly via session resumption or optimized cipher suites—can shave milliseconds off every request.
- **Optimizing DNS:** Users encountering DNS resolution delays can see significant slowdowns in page load times. Use global DNS providers with low-latency resolution or set TTL (time-to-live) values judiciously for ephemeral services.

7.3 Observability and Logging

Even the most finely tuned SaaS system will eventually encounter unexpected load spikes, latency outliers, or partial failures in upstream dependencies. **Observability** is the practice of designing systems whose operational states can be understood, measured, and debugged in real time. In this section, we describe the critical components of an observability stack—**logs**, **metrics**, and **traces**—and how to unify them into a coherent strategy for diagnosing and resolving performance issues quickly.

7.3.1 Distributed Tracing

Purpose and Concepts

Modern SaaS often embraces microservice or modular architectures, leading to a web of inter-service calls. A single user request can traverse multiple components (front-end gateway, backend microservices, database calls, external APIs), making it difficult to pinpoint which step is the bottleneck when latency spikes or errors occur.

- **Key Idea of Tracing:** Assign each incoming request a unique identifier (trace ID). As the request flows through different services, each service logs a "span" of time plus contextual data. By aggregating all spans under the same trace ID, you reconstruct the entire journey from start to finish.

Popular Tools

- **Jaeger and Zipkin:** Widely adopted open-source tracing solutions. They capture spans, store them in a backend, and provide UIs to visualize latencies across service boundaries.
- **OpenTelemetry:** A vendor-neutral initiative that defines telemetry collection for traces, metrics, and logs. By adopting OpenTelemetry, you decouple your instrumentation from a particular vendor solution.

Practices for Effective Tracing

1. **Automatic Instrumentation:** Many frameworks (Spring Boot, Express.js, Django) or languages provide instrumentation libraries that generate trace data automatically, eliminating the need for manual instrumentation in every function.
2. **Propagating Context:** Services must forward trace headers (like X-Trace-ID) in outbound calls so subsequent services can attach spans to the correct trace.
3. **Sampling Strategy:** Full tracing can be resource-heavy. You might sample only a percentage of requests or dynamically sample slow or error-prone ones.

7.3.2 Log Aggregation and Analysis

Logs are a foundational element of debugging and understanding runtime behavior, especially for incidents that may not manifest as clear performance anomalies in metrics.

1. **Centralized Logging:** Instead of storing logs locally on each container or VM, export them to a central platform (e.g., ELK Stack—Elasticsearch, Logstash, Kibana—or Splunk, Graylog). This approach ensures logs remain accessible even if instances are ephemeral or replaced.

2. **Structured Log Entries:** Adopt JSON or a similar structured format. This enables programmatic filtering and correlation across multiple fields (tenant ID, request path, error type).

3. **Severity Levels and Context:** Differentiate between DEBUG, INFO, WARN, and ERROR so you can filter logs by urgency. Also, include context such as request IDs, user identifiers, or relevant configuration states, making each log line more actionable.

4. **Indexing and Querying:** If your SaaS is large, logging volumes can be massive. Consider rolling indices, archive policies, or time-based retention. Tools like Kibana enable advanced queries (aggregations, time-based histograms), while custom dashboards can help reveal patterns or anomalies.

5. **Alerting from Logs:** Certain patterns in logs—like recurring errors with the same signature—may signal deeper performance or code issues. Configure triggers that generate alerts if these patterns exceed normal thresholds.

7.3.3 Real-Time Monitoring and Alerting

While logs and traces are invaluable for post-mortem or deep diagnostics, real-time performance issues require immediate detection and response.

- **Threshold Alerts:** For example, if the average response time climbs above 500ms for more than 5 minutes, send notifications to an on-call rotation.

- **Anomaly Detection:** Tools with AI or machine learning capabilities can detect subtle patterns that deviate from historical norms, flagging possible emergent problems.
- **Synthetic Monitoring:** Simulated user transactions from multiple geographic regions can confirm external availability and measure actual user experience. If the synthetic checks fail, you know that external customers are likely impacted.
- **Multi-Channel Notifications:** Alerts may route to Slack or Teams channels for immediate visibility, while critical ones can escalate to phone calls or PagerDuty pages for guaranteed human intervention.

7.3.4 Capacity Planning and Forecasting

Observability also informs your decisions about capacity expansions, environment tuning, or feature rollout schedules.

1. **Historical Usage Trends:** By analyzing multi-month data on CPU usage, memory consumption, RPS, and concurrency levels, you can predict the trajectory of resource needs.
2. **Load Testing:** Periodically simulating peak loads (like end-of-quarter usage surges or seasonal spikes) identifies potential performance hotspots. Synthetic load tests with your production-like environment can reveal whether an additional buffer is required.
3. **Budgeting and Infrastructure Provisioning:** Cloud environments typically allow you to scale up or out on demand. But cost forecasting becomes tricky if usage patterns are erratic. Observability can highlight cost drivers, enabling strategic architecture or resource tier changes.
4. **Feature Flagging for New Releases:** When rolling out new features, use feature flags to ramp up usage slowly, monitoring performance metrics. If the new feature degrades performance, you can roll back quickly before impacting the entire user base.

Chapter 8: SaaS Pricing Models and Business Strategies

SaaS companies face a unique challenge: how to transform their software offerings into profitable, sustainable businesses in a highly competitive, rapidly evolving market. More than just technology, success in SaaS hinges on finding the right pricing models, shaping compelling value propositions, and executing go-to-market strategies that drive growth and retain customers over the long term. In this chapter, we explore the ins and outs of **SaaS pricing**—from pay-as-you-go models to freemium approaches and tiered subscription plans—and delve into the **business strategies** that help convert prospective leads into loyal, profitable customers.

The stakes are high: your pricing not only defines how you generate revenue but also shapes your brand's market position and signals your platform's perceived value. Meanwhile, business strategies around customer acquisition, churn reduction, and expansion significantly influence sustainability, as do metrics like Lifetime Value (LTV) and Customer Acquisition Cost (CAC). Understanding and optimizing these components of a SaaS business model is crucial for achieving scalable growth, minimizing churn, and building long-term customer relationships.

8.1 SaaS Business Models

A well-structured business model lays the foundation for how your SaaS company creates, delivers, and captures value. While each SaaS product is unique, certain common patterns and frameworks have proven effective, from basic subscription packages to sophisticated usage-based pricing. In this section, we explore these core SaaS business models and examine how to choose the best approach for your product and market.

8.1.1 Subscription vs. Pay-as-You-Go

At the heart of SaaS lies a fundamental question: Should you charge customers a recurring subscription fee, or should you adopt a pay-as-you-go model that bills them based on actual usage?

Subscription Model

- **Definition and Characteristics:** In a pure subscription model, customers pay a fixed, recurring fee—often monthly or annually—to access the software. This fee may vary based on usage constraints, feature sets, or service tiers (such as Basic, Professional, and Enterprise), but the payment itself remains consistent at each billing cycle.
- **Advantages**
  1. **Predictable Revenue:** Subscriptions create more consistent and predictable revenue streams, facilitating accurate financial forecasting.
  2. **Ease of Budgeting for Customers:** Businesses appreciate fixed costs, making it straightforward for them to budget and justify renewing each period.
  3. **Alignment with Value-Added Services:** Subscription tiers can bundle features, premium support, or enhanced security to encourage customers to upgrade.

- **Challenges**
    1. **Overpay or Underuse Concerns:** Some customers may perceive that they're paying for features or capacity they don't need.
    2. **Limited Flexibility:** Customers with highly variable usage might prefer usage-based models for fairness and cost control.
    3. **Churn Risk at Renewal Points:** Each billing cycle is a moment when customers might re-evaluate whether to continue.

Pay-as-You-Go (Usage-Based) Model

- **Definition and Characteristics:** A pay-as-you-go model ties billing directly to consumption metrics (e.g., number of transactions, data processed, emails sent, or compute hours). Customers are invoiced for the exact resources or features consumed during a billing cycle.
- **Advantages**
    1. **Fairness and Transparency:** Customers pay only for what they use, improving perceived fairness and trust.
    2. **Encourages Low Barrier to Entry:** New users can start small at a minimal cost, potentially accelerating adoption.
    3. **Upside Potential:** As a customer's usage expands, revenue scales without negotiation for higher tiers.
- **Challenges**
    1. **Unpredictable Revenue:** Invoiced amounts can fluctuate significantly, complicating financial forecasting.
    2. **Customer Friction:** Some customers may prefer predictable subscription costs rather than variable invoices.

3. **Complex Billing Infrastructure:** Implementing precise usage tracking and billing can be technically challenging.

In practice, many SaaS providers blend these approaches. For instance, a base subscription might grant access to core features, with additional charges applied for usage beyond a predefined threshold. This hybrid approach can balance predictability and fairness, though it demands a robust billing system that can handle both subscription and usage-based charges.

8.1.2 Freemium and Tiered Pricing Models

For SaaS startups and established players alike, freemium and tiered pricing models offer unique ways to segment customers and entice them to adopt (and potentially upgrade) your software.

Freemium Model

- **Definition:** A freemium model provides limited functionality or usage of the software at no cost, with revenue generated from customers who opt for premium tiers.
- **Benefits**
    1. **Rapid User Acquisition:** By removing cost barriers, you encourage mass adoption. Once users are engaged, they may opt to upgrade for advanced features.
    2. **Brand Awareness:** Freemium can quickly elevate your brand recognition in a crowded market, especially if your free tier is generous enough to attract interest.
    3. **Product-Led Growth:** Freemium encourages product-led growth strategies where users drive your marketing by inviting peers or recommending your software.
- **Risks and Drawbacks**

1. **Conversion Rate Variability:** Not all free users will convert, and some may remain on the free plan indefinitely.
2. **Support Overheads:** Large numbers of free users can strain support resources if they expect help or training.
3. **Potential Undervaluation:** If the free tier offers too much value, some may see little reason to upgrade, diluting revenue potential.

Tiered Pricing

- **Definition:** In a tiered pricing structure, you offer multiple packages (for example, Basic, Standard, and Premium) with increasing levels of functionality, usage allowances, or support options.
- **Key Design Elements**
  1. **Feature Differentiation:** Each tier should unlock clear, value-added features that justify its higher price.
  2. **User Segmentation:** Align tiers with different customer segments (e.g., small businesses, mid-market, enterprises), reflecting their budgets and needs.
  3. **Upsell Opportunities:** By clearly showing how a higher tier offers more benefits, you encourage customers to upgrade as they grow or as their needs evolve.
- **Advantages**
  1. **Simplicity in Messaging:** Tiers make it straightforward for buyers to understand what they get at each price point.
  2. **Predictable Revenues:** Tiered pricing supports consistent subscription revenue, aiding financial projections.
  3. **Flexibility:** Additional add-ons can be incorporated— for instance, advanced analytics or VIP support—for an extra fee.

- **Potential Pitfalls**
  1. **Complicated Upgrades or Downgrades:** If transitions between tiers are cumbersome, customer frustration can lead to churn.
  2. **Customer Confusion:** Overly granular tiers (e.g., six or eight tiers) may overwhelm prospective buyers and slow the sales process.
  3. **Mispriced Tiers:** If the gap in value between tiers is too large, potential customers may either feel forced to overpay or perceive your offering as insufficient.

These pricing models can be combined: a SaaS provider might offer a freemium tier for individual users, a basic paid tier for SMBs, and more advanced enterprise tiers with dedicated support and compliance features. This flexibility allows you to capture different segments while preserving a logical upgrade path that fosters revenue growth.

8.1.3 Monetization and Billing Systems

Once you determine your pricing strategy—be it subscription-based, usage-based, freemium, or tiered—implementing a reliable, user-friendly monetization and billing system is imperative.

Building vs. Buying

- **Building In-House:** Some companies develop custom billing systems, granting full control over feature sets, data flow, and user experience. This approach demands dedicated engineering resources and ongoing maintenance but can be tailored precisely to your unique pricing model.
- **Third-Party Billing Providers:** Platforms like Stripe, Recurly, Chargebee, or Braintree offer robust billing engines that integrate subscription management, dunning (failed payment retry mechanisms), and analytics. Using these can drastically reduce development overhead and accelerate go-to-market, though customization might be limited.

Revenue Recognition and Compliance

- **Accounting Standards:** SaaS companies often operate under ASC 606 (U.S. GAAP) or IFRS 15 (internationally) for revenue recognition. Ensuring your billing system can handle complex scenarios (e.g., deferring revenue for annual subscriptions) is crucial for legal and financial compliance.
- **Tax Management:** Global SaaS vendors must handle sales tax, VAT, or GST across multiple jurisdictions. Solutions like TaxJar and Avalara integrate with billing systems to automate tax calculations.
- **Security and Data Privacy:** Storing credit card data and processing transactions require strict adherence to PCI DSS (Payment Card Industry Data Security Standard). If possible, offload this responsibility to PCI-compliant payment gateways.

Subscription Lifecycle and Dunning

- **Subscription Lifecycle Management:** A robust system monitors the entire customer lifecycle: from trial sign-up and free-tier usage to upgrades, renewals, and potential cancellations. Automated email campaigns can remind customers of expiring trials or upcoming renewals.
- **Dunning and Retention:** Dunning processes address failed payments by sending alerts, retrying charges, and suspending or downgrading accounts if payment issues remain unresolved. Effective dunning can recover revenue and reduce involuntary churn.

8.2 Customer Retention and Growth Strategies

In SaaS, growth doesn't just come from new sign-ups. Retaining existing customers and nurturing expansions within their accounts (e.g., seat expansions or additional service modules) can be even more profitable. Customer churn—the rate at which customers cancel or fail to renew—represents a direct loss of revenue, so minimizing it is a top priority. In this section, we delve into methods for reducing churn, fostering customer success, and maximizing lifetime value.

8.2.1 Churn Reduction Techniques

Churn refers to the percentage of customers who discontinue their subscriptions over a set period—monthly or annually. High churn quickly erodes your revenue base and undermines the value of your marketing and sales efforts.

1. Onboarding and Training

- **Comprehensive Onboarding:** Provide new users with guided tutorials, documentation, and initial setup wizards. Customers who rapidly see the value of your product are less likely to churn.
- **Interactive Walkthroughs:** Tools like Userpilot or Appcues enable in-app walkthroughs that guide users through key features. This approach ensures that user adoption is smooth and frictionless.
- **Knowledge Base and FAQ:** Maintain a detailed, easy-to-navigate knowledge base. When issues arise, customers should find clear, concise answers rapidly.

2. Customer Support and Success

- **Customer Success Teams:** Assign dedicated success managers to high-value customers. These professionals monitor product usage, recommend best practices, and proactively address concerns, reducing the likelihood of churn.
- **Responsive Support:** Provide multiple support channels—email, live chat, phone—and ensure quick, helpful responses. Poor support experiences are a leading cause of churn.

- **Proactive Outreach:** Use usage analytics to spot signs of dissatisfaction—such as dropping usage or negative feedback—and intervene early with personalized help or check-ins.

3. Value Engagement and Ongoing Communication

- **Regular Product Updates:** Communicate new features, improvements, and bug fixes. An active roadmap instills confidence that your product is continually evolving to meet user needs.
- **Newsletters and Webinars:** Share tips, best practices, and success stories. Engaging educational content can deepen product usage and loyalty.
- **Customer Communities:** Foster online forums or user groups where customers can share advice and troubleshoot together, thereby increasing engagement and building a sense of community.

4. Feedback Loops and Exit Surveys

- **Feedback Cycles:** Actively solicit feedback through in-app surveys or Net Promoter Score (NPS) assessments. Demonstrate that you listen and respond by prioritizing features that customers request.
- **Exit Surveys:** If a customer cancels, ask why. This information is invaluable for understanding product gaps, support deficiencies, or pricing concerns. Track recurring themes and prioritize improvements accordingly.

8.2.2 Scaling Sales and Customer Success

For SaaS companies, achieving scalable growth means systematizing your sales processes and ensuring that high-value accounts are nurtured for the long term.

Building a Sales Funnel

- **Lead Generation:** Leverage inbound marketing (content marketing, SEO, social media) and outbound efforts (cold outreach, events, partner networks) to fill the top of your funnel with qualified leads.
- **Lead Qualification:** Use scoring methods based on company size, industry, budget, and purchase intent to prioritize high-quality leads. Marketing automation tools (Marketo, HubSpot, Pardot) can streamline this process.
- **CRM and Pipeline Management:** Adopt a CRM solution (Salesforce, HubSpot CRM, Pipedrive) to track prospects from initial contact to close. Clear pipeline visibility helps predict revenue and allocate sales resources efficiently.

Customer Lifecycle Stages

1. **Prospecting:** Generating interest through marketing or referrals.
2. **Evaluation:** The customer tests your product via a trial or demo.
3. **Purchase:** The decision is made, and contracts are signed (if required).
4. **Onboarding:** Immediate focus on rapid value delivery and account setup.
5. **Adoption & Usage:** Encouraging deeper engagement with product features.
6. **Renewal or Expansion:** Moving the customer to higher tiers or cross-selling additional modules.
7. **Retention and Advocacy:** Satisfied customers become brand ambassadors.

Account Management and Expansion

- **Upselling and Cross-Selling:** Regular check-ins with existing customers can identify unmet needs that align with your premium tiers or complementary add-ons. This approach drives revenue expansion over time.

- **Enterprise and Custom Deals:** In B2B scenarios, large enterprises may require custom contract terms, compliance guarantees, or dedicated account managers. Tailoring your approach to these high-value prospects can significantly boost your average contract value (ACV).

- **Partnerships and Integrations:** Collaborate with other SaaS vendors or channel partners to provide integrated solutions. Co-marketing efforts can expand your reach and introduce your product to complementary customer bases.

8.2.3 Monetization and Billing Systems

While earlier we discussed the technical aspects of monetization, effectively capitalizing on expansions also demands strategic positioning of billing features. For example:

- **Seat-Based Expansion:** If you charge per user or seat, ensure that purchasing additional seats or unsubscribing from seats is frictionless.

- **Feature-Based Add-Ons:** Provide on-demand add-ons like advanced analytics, team collaboration tools, or professional services. Clear, transparent pricing encourages adoption without the hassle of renegotiating entire contracts.

- **Usage Threshold Notifications:** Alert customers when they approach or exceed usage limits. This proactive communication fosters trust and encourages timely upgrades, avoiding sticker shock on invoices.

8.3 Monetization and Billing Systems

Monetization and billing are central to capturing the revenue from all your pricing and customer success strategies. While you've already established pricing models, your ability to manage these models seamlessly can influence customer satisfaction and long-term retention.

8.3.1 Implementing a Billing System

A well-designed billing system does more than collect money; it shapes user perceptions, streamlines operations, and ensures compliance.

Requirements and Considerations

- **Multi-Currency Support:** Serving a global customer base may necessitate accepting multiple currencies. Currency conversion fluctuations must be handled gracefully, with transparent exchange rates or hedging strategies for extended contracts.

- **Recurring Billing and Invoicing:** Automate recurring billing and provide downloadable invoices or receipts for each billing cycle. This establishes trust and reduces support queries.

- **Payment Gateways and Methods:** Integrate multiple payment gateways (e.g., Stripe, PayPal, Adyen) to give customers flexibility. In enterprise contexts, you may need to support wire transfers or purchase orders as well.

- **API Integrations:** A robust billing system should expose APIs that let you embed billing interactions into your SaaS platform, enabling frictionless upgrades, downgrades, and payment updates within the customer's account dashboard.

Reporting and Analytics

- **Revenue Attribution:** Understanding which features or marketing campaigns drive paid conversions is critical for resource allocation. Break down revenue by product line, region, or sales channel to glean strategic insights.

- **Cohort Analysis:** Examine how certain user cohorts (e.g., signups from a specific month) behave over time. Do they upgrade, churn, or show more usage patterns that lead to expansions? Cohort analysis provides essential data for refining both product design and sales strategy.
- **MRR and ARR Tracking:** Monthly Recurring Revenue (MRR) and Annual Recurring Revenue (ARR) are foundational metrics in SaaS. Automated tracking of these metrics helps you spot trends and evaluate the impact of strategic initiatives like new pricing tiers or upsell campaigns.

8.3.2 Revenue Recognition and Compliance

Proper revenue recognition is not just an accounting formality; it's a regulatory requirement that impacts investor confidence and creditworthiness.

ASC 606 / IFRS 15 Considerations

- **Subscription Revenue:** Typically recognized ratably over the subscription period. If customers pay annually, revenue is deferred and then recognized monthly.
- **Variable Consideration:** For usage-based billing, revenue recognition may fluctuate based on monthly usage, requiring additional accounting processes.
- **Multi-Element Arrangements:** When a SaaS deal includes professional services, hardware, or third-party licenses, each element might need to be separated and recognized over distinct timelines.

Tax and Regulatory Concerns

- **Sales Tax and VAT:** Each jurisdiction may have different rules for applying taxes to digital services. Ensure your billing system can handle tax calculations automatically, potentially with external services for real-time rates.

- **E-Invoicing Regulations:** Some regions require electronic invoices that adhere to government standards or are reported to tax authorities. Maintaining compliance prevents legal complications.
- **Data Protection Laws:** Billing systems handle sensitive financial data. Implement robust encryption, tokenization, and compliance with data protection regulations (e.g., GDPR) to safeguard user data and maintain trust.

8.3.3 Advanced Revenue Strategies

As your SaaS platform matures, explore advanced revenue strategies that go beyond simple subscriptions.

Partnership Ecosystems

- **Resellers and White-Labeling:** Building reseller relationships can expand your reach into new markets. White-label options enable partners to rebrand your solution while paying you a licensing or usage fee.
- **Co-Marketing Initiatives:** Collaborate with complementary SaaS solutions, bundling features to create a more comprehensive offering for customers.

Platform Monetization

- **Marketplace and Ecosystem:** If you have a robust platform, consider launching an app marketplace where third-party developers can create plugins or integrations. Revenue can come from listing fees, revenue sharing, or transaction fees.
- **Data-as-a-Service (DaaS):** In certain markets, anonymized data insights can be monetized if done ethically and in compliance with data protection laws. This model requires a clear value proposition and robust privacy controls.

Pricing Experiments and Optimization

- **A/B Testing and Price Sensitivity:** Deploy controlled experiments to test different price points, discount offers, or feature bundling. Gather empirical data before permanently changing your pricing structure.
- **Dynamic Pricing:** In some scenarios, real-time factors like demand or seasonal usage patterns can inform dynamic pricing. While complex to implement, it can maximize revenue if done transparently.
- **Localized Pricing:** Adjust price points for different regions or countries to align with local purchasing power. This approach helps capture global markets without alienating price-sensitive regions.

Chapter 9: Migration and Integration in SaaS

In the broader arc of SaaS adoption, migration and integration stand out as two of the most complex and resource-intensive endeavors. Organizations seeking to shift from on-premises or legacy hosted applications to SaaS often find themselves navigating a tangle of data-transfer challenges, user acceptance hurdles, and technical constraints. Simultaneously, once established in a SaaS model, companies must integrate their new cloud-based systems with a variety of applications—both internal and external—to ensure seamless workflows and data consistency.

This chapter explores the migration and integration lifecycle in a SaaS context, outlining best practices, risk mitigation strategies, and design patterns that can help you execute these initiatives effectively. We begin by examining the intricacies of moving legacy applications to a SaaS environment, considering the various phased approaches and big-bang migrations, and highlighting the organizational factors that often dictate success or failure. We then delve into the fundamentals of API integration—comparing RESTful and GraphQL paradigms and detailing webhook- and event-driven models—before turning to the specific challenges of integrating SaaS platforms with third-party services like CRMs, payment gateways, and analytics solutions. Finally, we address practical concerns such as managing API rate limits and ensuring reliability under heavy loads or complex traffic patterns.

By the end of this chapter, you should have a deep appreciation of the nuances involved in migrating and integrating SaaS applications— from the earliest planning stages through post-deployment optimization—and be equipped with the tools and knowledge to tackle these undertakings head-on.

9.1 Migrating Legacy Applications to SaaS

One of the biggest hurdles in SaaS adoption is the transition from legacy on-premises or custom-hosted solutions to a cloud-based, multi-tenant environment. This journey requires careful planning, cross-functional coordination, and an in-depth understanding of both the existing system and the target SaaS platform. Migration does not merely involve transferring data; it frequently entails rethinking processes, refactoring or rewriting application logic, and guiding end users through significant changes in workflow.

9.1.1 Challenges and Strategies

Moving to a SaaS model often brings considerable benefits in cost structure, scalability, and maintenance overhead. However, the path to these advantages is fraught with pitfalls that can undermine your entire digital transformation effort. Below are several challenges and the high-level strategies you can employ to address them:

Organizational and Cultural Barriers

- **Resistance to Change:** Departments or individuals may be highly invested in the status quo of a legacy system, viewing the SaaS transition as unnecessary or disruptive. Overcoming this mindset requires comprehensive communication, stakeholder alignment, and targeted training initiatives.

- **Skill Gaps:** Managing and developing SaaS applications often demand different skill sets than traditional on-premises solutions. Your IT team may need new competencies in cloud orchestration, subscription billing, or multi-tenant data models.

- **Executive Buy-In:** Without strong executive sponsorship and budgetary support, large-scale migrations can stall during unanticipated difficulties. Gaining leadership endorsement is crucial to sustaining momentum across departmental lines.

Technical Hurdles

- **Complex Data Models:** Legacy applications can harbor convoluted schemas or proprietary data formats that must be carefully mapped to a SaaS-friendly structure. Data cleanup and transformation can be one of the most time-consuming aspects of the migration.

- **Dependencies and Integrations:** Existing systems rarely operate in isolation. They may rely on specialized hardware, licensed software libraries, or custom integration with other corporate systems. Replacing or replicating these dependencies in a SaaS environment can be difficult.

- **Performance Considerations:** Workloads that rely heavily on low-latency local networks, batch processing, or near real-time updates may need architecture adjustments in the SaaS model. Cloud providers often have different performance characteristics than local data centers.

Compliance and Security Constraints

- **Regulatory Environment:** Industries like finance, healthcare, or government face stringent regulations regarding data residency, encryption, and auditing. Migrating to a SaaS platform could require specialized compliance certifications (e.g., HIPAA, FedRAMP, PCI DSS).

- **Risk Assessment and Governance:** Corporate risk officers and compliance teams often scrutinize SaaS providers' security and operational policies. The migration plan must address these concerns, potentially requiring contract clauses or additional validations.

- **Data Privacy:** Storing customer or employee data in the cloud can raise privacy questions, particularly if multiple tenants share the underlying infrastructure. Meticulous tenant isolation and robust encryption at rest and in transit are essential to maintaining trust.

High-Level Migration Strategies

These challenges typically converge into a few widely adopted approaches:

1. **Lift-and-Shift (Rehost):** Easiest in concept, a lift-and-shift strategy moves an application to the cloud with minimal modifications. This can expedite migration, but the resulting application might not leverage cloud-native features or multi-tenancy optimizations.

2. **Partial Refactoring (Replatform):** Certain parts of the legacy application are modified to be more cloud-friendly—such as replacing on-premises dependencies or adopting container orchestration—while preserving a fair portion of the original code.

3. **Full Refactoring or Re-Architecting:** An older system is substantially rewritten or redesigned to take advantage of multi-tenant SaaS capabilities, scaling, and microservices. This approach is more resource-intensive but yields significant long-term benefits.

4. **Repurchasing or Replacing:** In some cases, it may be more cost-effective to replace a legacy system with a new SaaS product that already fulfills most business requirements. This approach can reduce maintenance overhead but requires data migration and significant change management.

Determining which strategy works best depends on factors like business urgency, budget, the longevity of the legacy system, and the degree of architectural mismatch between the old and new environments. Often, organizations blend these strategies—migrating some functions via lift-and-shift while simultaneously refactoring high-impact modules for optimal SaaS performance.

9.1.2 Phased vs. Big Bang Migration

Equally critical to "what" you migrate is "how" you choose to sequence the migration. While some organizations opt for a "Big Bang" cutover where they switch everything to SaaS at once, others adopt a more measured, phased approach that spreads the risk over time.

Phased Migration

- **Description:**
  You move discrete modules or user groups to the SaaS platform in stages, gradually expanding usage until the entire system is cloud-based.
- **Advantages:**

1. **Lower Risk:** If a particular phase encounters issues, they can be contained without impacting the entire enterprise.
2. **Incremental Learning:** Each completed phase yields lessons that inform subsequent phases, refining your migration processes.
3. **User Acceptance:** Phased rollouts allow end users to adapt gradually, minimizing the shock of wholesale changes.

- **Drawbacks:**

1. **Longer Timelines:** Dividing the migration into multiple stages can significantly extend the total project duration.
2. **Interim Complexity:** Both the new SaaS system and the legacy environment must coexist, often requiring complex "bridges" or integration layers.
3. **Potential Duplication of Effort:** Some tasks (like environment setup or vendor negotiations) may be repeated across phases.

Big Bang Migration

- **Description:**
  In a Big Bang approach, you plan a single switchover date after preparing the SaaS environment, migrating data, and training users. The legacy system is then decommissioned (or frozen) simultaneously.
- **Advantages:**

1. **Speed of Completion:** Once the cutover is complete, you can invest fully in optimizing your SaaS solution without continuously maintaining two environments.

2. **Reduced Complexity:** You avoid having to synchronize data and operations between old and new systems over an extended period.
3. **Clear Milestones:** The entire organization is aligned around one major event, potentially simplifying communications.

- **Drawbacks:**

1. **Higher Risk Exposure:** If critical flaws emerge at cutover, the organization could face system-wide downtime or operational chaos.
2. **User Resistance:** A large-scale transition can intimidate end users, potentially exacerbating adoption barriers if they're unprepared for radical changes.
3. **Burden on IT Resources:** The IT team must ensure absolute readiness by the switchover date, often under intense pressure to meet unmovable deadlines.

Most enterprises choose a hybrid approach that phases in some major components while orchestrating a Big Bang cutover for smaller or less critical modules. Balancing risk, cost, and speed is key. Regardless of the method, rigorous testing, stakeholder engagement, and thorough contingency planning form the backbone of any successful SaaS migration.

9.2 API Integration in SaaS

Once migrated or adopted, the effectiveness of a SaaS solution often hinges on how well it integrates with other systems. In many organizations, SaaS platforms function as part of a larger software ecosystem, communicating with on-premises databases, other cloud services, or external vendor APIs. Failing to establish reliable, secure, and scalable integrations can undercut the potential benefits of SaaS—slowing workflows, duplicating data, and introducing error-prone manual workarounds.

9.2.1 RESTful vs. GraphQL APIs

APIs are the linchpin of SaaS integrations. They define the contracts by which data is created, read, updated, and deleted (CRUD) across different applications. Two major paradigms for SaaS APIs dominate: **REST** and **GraphQL**.

RESTful APIs

- **Core Concepts:** REST (Representational State Transfer) is an architectural style that uses standard HTTP methods (GET, POST, PUT, DELETE) to access resources identified by unique URIs. RESTful APIs typically return JSON or XML, often with predictable data structures and status codes.
- **Advantages for SaaS Integrations:**
  1. **Simplicity and Familiarity:** Developers worldwide recognize REST conventions, making it easy to onboard new teams or third-party partners.
  2. **Statelessness:** The server does not track client state, making horizontal scaling straightforward in a SaaS environment.
  3. **Fine-Grained Caching and CDN Support:** Because REST uses standard HTTP verbs, caching solutions can optimize repeated GET requests effectively.
- **Potential Limitations:**
  1. **Over-Fetching or Under-Fetching:** REST endpoints may return large payloads that clients don't need, or clients may need multiple requests to gather related data.
  2. **Complex Endpoints:** Over time, a proliferation of resource types and versioning can complicate endpoint management.

GraphQL

- **Core Concepts:** GraphQL is a query language and runtime that allows clients to request precisely the data they need, in a single request. GraphQL servers expose schemas describing types and relationships, enabling clients to craft queries that retrieve multiple, nested resources simultaneously.
- **Advantages for SaaS Integrations:**
  1. **Flexible Data Retrieval:** Clients can reduce over-fetching by specifying only needed fields. This is beneficial for bandwidth or performance-sensitive scenarios.
  2. **Single Endpoint:** GraphQL typically uses one endpoint (/graphql), simplifying network configuration and allowing dynamic queries.
  3. **Introspection and Strong Typing:** Built-in schema documentation fosters a self-explanatory integration experience, especially for third parties.
- **Potential Limitations:**
  1. **Complex Caching:** Because queries are often dynamic, caching responses at the HTTP layer is trickier.
  2. **Higher Server Complexity:** GraphQL resolvers require more sophisticated handling of relationships and performance optimization.
  3. **Learning Curve:** Teams accustomed to REST may need time to adapt to GraphQL's schema-based approach.

When designing a SaaS API, the decision between RESTful and GraphQL paradigms often hinges on developer preference, the nature of the data, and the complexity of expected queries. In many cases, a RESTful approach remains sufficient, especially for straightforward resource-based integrations or legacy systems. GraphQL can shine in scenarios where clients require highly customized data sets or must minimize round trips. Some SaaS providers offer both interfaces, giving integrators a choice.

9.2.2 Webhooks and Event-Driven Integrations

Beyond request-response APIs, modern SaaS solutions frequently use **webhooks** or event-driven integrations to handle asynchronous workflows. In such scenarios, the SaaS application broadcasts events (e.g., "new user created," "order paid," "analysis completed") to external systems, which can then respond or trigger follow-up actions.

Webhooks

- **Definition and Workflow:** A webhook is a callback mechanism where the SaaS platform sends an HTTP POST request to a specified endpoint whenever a particular event occurs. The receiving endpoint processes the payload in real time.
- **Common Use Cases:**
    1. **Real-Time Notifications:** E-commerce applications can notify external systems of payment status changes.
    2. **Continuous Integration:** Developer-focused SaaS tools may trigger build pipelines on code repository events.
    3. **Data Sync:** Whenever a new record is created in the SaaS system, webhooks automatically update external databases.
- **Implementation Considerations:**
    1. **Security:** Validate incoming webhook calls (e.g., via signature headers) to prevent spoofing. Use HTTPS for data confidentiality.
    2. **Reliability:** The receiving endpoint could be down or slow. SaaS providers often implement retries with backoff or queueing to ensure event delivery.
    3. **Scalability:** A high volume of webhook events requires load balancing and robust architecture to handle bursts of traffic.

Event-Driven Architectures

- **Message Buses and Pub/Sub:** Instead of directly calling an HTTP endpoint, some SaaS products publish events to a message broker like Kafka or AWS SNS, from which subscribers can consume and process them. This reduces direct coupling between the SaaS provider and integrators.
- **Benefits of Event-Driven Integration:**
    1. **Loose Coupling:** The SaaS platform doesn't need to know how each subscriber processes events, easing changes on either side.
    2. **Resilience:** If an endpoint is temporarily unavailable, the message queue can buffer events until it recovers.
    3. **Scalability:** Multiple consumers can subscribe to the same event topic, distributing tasks across separate worker processes.
- **Challenges:**
    1. **Complex Setup:** Implementing brokers and managing subscriber identities can be more intricate than straightforward webhooks.
    2. **Guaranteed Delivery:** Some protocols offer "at least once" delivery, which can lead to duplicate event processing unless carefully handled.

For many SaaS use cases, webhooks suffice to provide near-real-time notifications without requiring integrators to poll the API. However, high-throughput or mission-critical scenarios may benefit from a more formal, event-driven architecture using publish/subscribe patterns. Each approach should be evaluated based on your platform's scale, reliability needs, and developer ecosystem.

9.3 Third-Party Service Integration

In the SaaS domain, delivering a seamless end-to-end experience often requires integrating with other platforms and services that customers already use—ranging from customer relationship management (CRM) and payment gateways to analytics engines and ERP systems.

Executing these integrations efficiently can be a competitive differentiator, as businesses often select a SaaS product that readily works alongside their existing software arsenal.

9.3.1 CRM, Payment Gateways, and Analytics

Let's explore some of the most common third-party services that SaaS solutions integrate with, highlighting best practices and potential pitfalls.

CRM Integrations

- **Rationale and Examples:** Tools like Salesforce, HubSpot CRM, or Microsoft Dynamics 365 house critical customer data, sales pipelines, and service workflows. SaaS products that manage user profiles, subscriptions, or orders can benefit from synchronizing data with a CRM to enable a unified view of the customer across marketing, sales, and support.

- **Key Design Considerations:**
  1. **Identity Mapping:** Determine how to match records between the CRM and the SaaS application (e.g., user email, account ID). Maintaining consistent identifiers prevents duplication or mismatch.
  2. **Update Frequency and Triggers:** Decide whether updates occur in real time (via webhooks) or in scheduled batches. More frequent updates can improve data accuracy but increase API traffic.
  3. **Field Mapping and Custom Objects:** CRMs often allow custom fields or objects. The integration logic must account for these customizations, ensuring that important data is not lost.
- **Common Pitfalls:**

1. **Rate Limit Exceedance:** CRMs typically have API rate limits, so synchronous batch operations can quickly exceed them if not carefully managed.
2. **Bidirectional Sync Complexity:** Keeping data aligned in both directions requires conflict-resolution rules to handle updates from multiple sources.
3. **Security & Permissions:** Integrations must respect CRM access controls, ensuring that only authorized data is exchanged.

Payment Gateways

- **Rationale and Examples:** For SaaS solutions that handle subscription billing or e-commerce transactions, integrating with payment processors like Stripe, PayPal, or Braintree is a necessity. These gateways manage credit card storage, transaction authorization, refunds, and more.

- **Integration Flows:**
  1. **Subscription Billing:** The SaaS platform can send subscription details (plan, price, billing cycle) to the gateway, which charges customers accordingly. Updates to payment methods or subscription cancellations must flow back to the SaaS.
  2. **One-Time Purchases:** For a single purchase model, an order is created in the SaaS system, and a payment token is requested from the gateway. On successful payment, the SaaS finalizes the order.
  3. **Webhooks for Payment Events:** Payment gateways typically send notifications (e.g., "payment failed," "charge succeeded"), allowing SaaS to react by suspending access or sending receipts.
- **Complexities:**

1. **Fraud Prevention:** Some gateways offer advanced fraud detection. The SaaS must handle scenarios where transactions are flagged or require additional verification.
2. **Multi-Currency Support:** If the SaaS operates globally, currency conversions and localized taxes can complicate integration.
3. **PCI Compliance:** Storing raw credit card data is heavily regulated. Relying on tokenization and hosted payment forms can alleviate compliance burdens.

Analytics and BI Tools

- **Rationale and Examples:** Many businesses rely on specialized analytics solutions (e.g., Google Analytics, Mixpanel, Looker, Tableau) for deeper insights. By integrating data from the SaaS platform, they can track user behavior, usage metrics, and key performance indicators.

- **Integration Patterns:**
  1. **Data Export:** Periodically exporting usage logs or aggregated data to a data warehouse or an analytics engine.
  2. **Real-Time Streaming:** Stream events (e.g., "user logged in," "item purchased") to analytics services like Segment or Snowplow for immediate processing.
  3. **Custom Dashboards:** Some SaaS products embed analytics capabilities within their own interface by connecting to BI APIs.
- **Challenges:**

  1. **Data Privacy and Governance:** Only share necessary data and respect user opt-outs or privacy regulations.

2. **Performance Overheads:** Overly granular analytics can produce high data volumes, increasing overhead and storage costs.

3. **Cohesive Data Model:** Mismatched naming conventions or incomplete data contexts reduce the quality of insights. Careful schema design improves clarity.

By thoughtfully designing these integrations, SaaS providers can deliver robust functionality that meshes seamlessly with their customers' existing software ecosystems. This level of interoperability can boost user satisfaction and serve as a key competitive advantage in crowded markets.

9.3.2 Managing API Rate Limits and Reliability

When integrating with or exposing external APIs, **rate limits** and **reliability** concerns surface frequently, especially for SaaS platforms operating at scale. API traffic can spike unpredictably, and each integration point is a potential point of failure.

Understanding Rate Limits

- **Definition:**
  Rate limits cap how many requests can be made to an API within a given time interval. Typical patterns might allow 100 requests per minute or 1,000 requests per day, though each provider sets unique policies.

- **Why They Matter:**
  Rate limits protect an API from abuse or DDoS-like traffic, but they can also inadvertently throttle legitimate customers if usage surges unexpectedly or batch jobs run too frequently.

- **Strategies to Mitigate Rate Limit Exceedance:**

1. **Client-Side Throttling:** Integrations can implement queues or backoff mechanisms to pace requests.
2. **Batching Requests:** Combine multiple operations into fewer calls if the API supports such batch endpoints.
3. **Caching:** Cache frequent responses to minimize redundant requests.
4. **Prioritizing Endpoints:** For mission-critical calls, ensure they have dedicated throughput, while less critical calls can be postponed.

Ensuring Reliability and High Availability

- **Circuit Breaker Patterns:** If external API calls repeatedly fail or time out, the circuit breaker opens and prevents further calls, giving the external service time to recover. This protects your SaaS from cascading failures that degrade the entire application.

- **Load Balancing:** Distributing requests across multiple nodes or endpoints can mitigate latency spikes or localized outages. If the external service offers multiple regional endpoints, a multi-regional approach can reduce latency for global tenants.

- **Retries and Backoff:** For transient errors (e.g., 503 server unavailable), automated retries with exponential backoff can salvage successful responses without overloading the server. However, ensure idempotence so repeated calls don't cause double-charging or duplicated actions.

- **Monitoring and Alerting:** Integrations must be monitored just like internal components. Metrics such as average response time, error rate, and success ratio help pinpoint where user-facing slowdowns or failures originate. Setting up alerts for anomalies ensures the DevOps team can intervene promptly.

- **Failover Strategies:** In some cases, the SaaS platform might maintain alternate endpoints or fallback logic. For example, if a primary payment gateway is down, you might route transactions through a secondary gateway.

Planning for Growth

- **Scaling with Multi-Tenancy:** As a SaaS provider takes on more tenants, traffic to integrated APIs can balloon. Preemptively negotiating higher rate limits or best-effort SLA expansions with critical partners ensures your platform can scale without abrupt, business-halting throttling.

- **Versioning and Lifecycle Management:** Third-party APIs evolve over time, sometimes deprecating endpoints or introducing new authentication flows. A robust integration strategy includes versioning support, proactive communication with vendor roadmaps, and a plan for transitioning tenants to updated endpoints with minimal disruption.

By carefully handling rate limits, reliability patterns, and ongoing version management, SaaS organizations can not only deliver stable, high-performance integrations but also maintain strong relationships with third-party providers—relationships that often directly impact user satisfaction and business continuity.

Chapter 10: Future Trends in SaaS Architecture

10.1 AI and Machine Learning in SaaS

Artificial Intelligence (AI) and Machine Learning (ML) have already begun reshaping the software landscape, and SaaS is no exception. Over the next few years, we can expect these technologies to become not only prevalent but deeply entwined with core SaaS offerings. While previous eras of SaaS focused on delivering software via the cloud with strong reliability and multi-tenant efficiency, the upcoming phase will emphasize **intelligent capabilities**—enabling SaaS platforms to learn from data at scale, automate complex tasks, and provide deeply personalized experiences.

10.1.1 AI-Driven Personalization

Context and Rationale

Personalization is fast becoming a critical competitive differentiator for SaaS providers. In industries ranging from retail to healthcare, users want software that proactively adapts to their behavior, role, or organizational context. Rather than offering a one-size-fits-all interface, SaaS applications can leverage AI to craft dynamic experiences—such as personalized dashboards, recommended actions, or specialized workflows. As the software acquires more data from user interactions, it can identify patterns and continuously refine its suggestions, much like consumer apps do with product recommendations or curated news feeds.

Technical Underpinnings

1. **User Behavior Modeling:** Personalization in SaaS typically starts with capturing user interaction data—clickstreams, navigation paths, feature usage metrics—and storing it in analytics pipelines. Machine learning algorithms (e.g., collaborative filtering, neural networks) then analyze this data to identify patterns in user behavior. SaaS providers can cluster users with similar usage profiles, enabling them to tailor experiences or recommend advanced features they might find valuable.

2. **Dynamic User Interfaces:** Front-end frameworks can be designed to handle dynamic layout changes or content blocks that are populated by a recommendation engine. These engines might run in real time (using microservices capable of sub-second inference) or on a scheduled basis (e.g., generating daily recommendations). SaaS architects must plan for how personalization logic interfaces with user session data and micro frontends—ensuring changes do not disrupt the user's workflow if updated asynchronously.

3. **Contextual Rules and Customization:** AI-based personalization should not eliminate user autonomy. Instead, it can be augmented by an administrative rules engine that allows enterprise customers to override or refine recommendations.

For instance, an HR SaaS platform might automatically suggest training modules for employees but give HR managers the ability to define mandatory modules or filter out certain topics based on corporate policies.

User Adoption and Ethical Considerations

- **Privacy and Compliance:** Personalized SaaS solutions rely heavily on user data. Providers must handle this data responsibly to avoid breaching regulations such as GDPR or CCPA. Clear user consent mechanisms and robust data anonymization techniques are vital.

- **User Trust:** Overly aggressive or irrelevant "recommendations" can backfire, causing user frustration. Striking a balance between helpful suggestions and user control is paramount. Including transparent explanations of why certain actions or features are recommended can increase trust.

- **Customization vs. Complexity:** While personalization can boost engagement, some enterprise users may prefer uniform experiences for compliance or training reasons. Offering toggles to enable or disable certain recommendation modules helps address these diverse needs.

10.1.2 Predictive Analytics and Automation

From Descriptive to Predictive

Traditional SaaS applications primarily focused on descriptive analytics: generating dashboards and visualizations of historical data. However, future SaaS architectures will heavily incorporate **predictive** and **prescriptive** analytics, using machine learning models to forecast outcomes, detect anomalies, and automate tasks based on probable future conditions.

1. **Predictive Maintenance and Forecasting:** Many SaaS offerings, especially those serving supply chain or manufacturing contexts, use AI to predict equipment failures, forecast demand, or schedule maintenance proactively. By tapping into streaming IoT data or historical usage metrics, predictive models identify patterns that signal impending bottlenecks or malfunctions.

2. **Risk Scoring and Fraud Detection:** In financial and insurance SaaS solutions, ML models can flag high-risk transactions or suspicious user behaviors. For instance, an e-invoicing SaaS might automatically halt or investigate anomalies like sudden spikes in invoice amounts from new payees. This level of intelligence significantly reduces operational overhead and manual verification.

3. **Automated Workflows:** AI-driven workflows go beyond passive alerts. They can autonomously trigger remediation steps or orchestrate cross-service actions. For instance, if a SaaS HR platform predicts an uptick in employee churn for a department (based on historical patterns of sick leave, performance data, or job satisfaction surveys), it can automatically schedule targeted training sessions or manager reviews.

ML-Ops for SaaS

To sustain predictive analytics at scale, SaaS providers must invest in **ML-Ops**—the discipline of operationalizing machine learning models. This includes:

- **Model Versioning:** As new data becomes available and models are retrained, version control ensures old predictions are traceable, facilitating audits and compliance.

- **Continuous Monitoring:** Predictive models degrade when data distributions shift. Monitoring real-time performance metrics (like accuracy, recall, or false positives) helps data scientists detect drift and schedule retraining.

- **Deployment Pipelines:** Deploying ML models in a SaaS environment may require specialized infrastructure for GPU acceleration or serverless inference. Tools like Kubeflow, MLflow, or proprietary cloud ML pipelines can automate packaging and scaling of models.

- **Explainability and Ethics:** Business buyers often demand that ML-driven decisions be interpretable, especially in regulated industries. Techniques like LIME (Local Interpretable Model-Agnostic Explanations) or SHAP (SHapley Additive exPlanations) can clarify how a model reached its conclusion, enhancing trust and compliance readiness.

Implications and Future Directions

As SaaS providers embed AI deeper into their workflows, they will blur the line between "software as a service" and "expert system as a service." Automated ticket triage in helpdesks, real-time revenue forecasting in e-commerce, and dynamic resource allocation in large-scale distributed apps are just the tip of the iceberg. The next phase will likely see **multi-modal AI** (combining text, image, and sensor data) and advanced **reinforcement learning** approaches that enable SaaS to adapt more fluidly to evolving contexts. Organizations that get ahead of this trend will find their SaaS solutions increasingly indispensable to end users.

10.2 Edge Computing for SaaS

Another future-shaping factor for SaaS is the continued rise of **edge**

computing. While the traditional SaaS model relies heavily on large, centralized data centers in the public cloud, new use cases demand that processing happen closer to end devices. From IoT-driven scenarios (e.g., factory floors, retail beacons) to latency-sensitive applications (e.g., real-time analytics, AR/VR), edge computing helps meet performance and data locality requirements that the mainstream SaaS approach does not always address well.

10.2.1 Reducing Latency with Edge Computing

Why Edge Matters

In certain domains—such as autonomous vehicles, industrial automation, or remote healthcare—mere milliseconds can be critical. Forwarding every piece of data to a distant cloud region introduces latency that might break the real-time constraints or degrade user experiences. Edge computing places compute and storage nodes at the "edge" of the network, physically nearer to sensors, devices, or local user clusters.

1. **Local Processing:** Instead of shipping raw sensor data to the cloud, edge nodes can perform initial filtering, aggregation, or anomaly detection. This lowers network bandwidth usage and improves response times.

2. **Offline Resilience:** Edge compute can handle tasks even when internet connectivity is intermittent or unreliable. For example, a SaaS platform managing remote wind farms might rely on local edge nodes to run control algorithms in the event of a connectivity disruption, syncing with the central cloud once the link is restored.

3. **Real-Time Interactions:** Consumer-facing SaaS, especially in gaming or immersive AR contexts, benefits significantly from local compute. An edge server close to players can host

partial logic or game session data, minimizing round-trip times and latency spikes.

Edge Integration Models for SaaS

- **Tiered Architecture:** A multi-tiered approach can place ephemeral microservices or caching layers at the edge, while core logic remains in a central cloud region. This preserves the global multi-tenant data while enhancing local performance.

- **Container Orchestration at the Edge:** Tools like Kubernetes can extend to edge environments, allowing SaaS providers to deploy scaled-down pods or container sets directly onto local clusters. This approach, however, brings challenges in cluster management, version control, and security across distributed endpoints.

- **Serverless Edge Functions:** Some cloud vendors now offer serverless runtimes that run at edge locations—an example is Cloudflare Workers. SaaS developers can deploy small code snippets that handle requests with minimal overhead. These "edge functions" excel at tasks like input validation, rewriting requests, or handling personal data locally for compliance reasons.

10.2.2 Hybrid Cloud and Edge Scenarios

While edge computing is often associated with a single cloud vendor's globally distributed infrastructure, an increasing number of organizations are adopting **hybrid cloud** strategies, combining private data centers, public cloud regions, and edge nodes into a unified environment. SaaS vendors seeking to accommodate these complex environments must adapt accordingly.

Hybrid Deployment Patterns

1. **Local Data Processing + Central Coordination:** The "edge" components handle real-time tasks and cache data, while a central SaaS cloud aggregates global analytics, handles multi-tenant logic, and orchestrates system-wide updates. This approach can significantly reduce bandwidth usage and enhance resilience.

2. **Geo-Distributed Microservices:** Large enterprises that require data sovereignty or compliance in multiple geographies may run microservices across different regions or private data centers. A carefully designed traffic management layer routes user requests to the nearest or most compliant location.

3. **Federated Learning:** In advanced AI scenarios, raw data remains local (for privacy or bandwidth reasons), but model updates are aggregated in a central server. This technique, known as federated learning, allows SaaS solutions to harness user data from multiple edges while keeping sensitive information local.

Operational Complexities

- **Observability and Diagnostics:** Monitoring a fleet of edge nodes demands more sophisticated telemetry collection, logs shipping, and distributed tracing. Traditional single-region dashboards might not scale. SaaS providers must adopt hierarchical or multi-tenant observability solutions that unify data from hundreds or thousands of edge sites.

- **Security at the Edge:** Edge nodes can be more vulnerable to physical tampering or local network intrusion. SaaS solutions need to integrate tamper-proof hardware modules, robust authentication, and cryptographic protocols to protect data in these   untrusted   environments.

- **Data Consistency:** In a scenario where user data can be partially stored at the edge and partially in the cloud, ensuring consistency is non-trivial. Techniques such as eventual consistency, CRDTs (Conflict-free Replicated Data Types), or local transactions with asynchronous synchronization might be required for distributed state management.

By embracing edge computing, SaaS vendors can unlock new markets and use cases that would otherwise be hindered by latency, data sovereignty, or connectivity constraints. As more devices generate real-time data, and users demand near-instant feedback, distributing some portion of SaaS logic closer to them becomes a critical differentiator.

10.3 No-Code and Low-Code SaaS Platforms

While AI and edge computing address complexity at deep technical levels, another major trend is the **democratization of software development** via no-code and low-code platforms. These solutions enable business analysts, domain experts, and even end users to create or modify SaaS workflows without extensive programming knowledge. As the global shortage of developer talent persists, low-code/no-code platforms can expedite project timelines, reduce costs, and empower more stakeholders to shape the software they rely on.

10.3.1 Benefits and Use Cases

Reduced Development Bottlenecks

Traditionally, implementing new features or customizing an existing SaaS solution demanded specialized coding skills. Low-code/no-code platforms abstract complex code behind visual interfaces (drag-and-drop components, prebuilt logic blocks) and form-based configuration. This significantly lowers the barrier for building line-of-business applications and prototypes, especially in small to medium-sized organizations where IT resources are often limited.

1. **Rapid Prototyping:** Departments can quickly mock up new modules or workflows for internal validation—an HR department might build an onboarding checklist, or a sales team might create a lead-scoring pipeline. If these prototypes prove successful, they can be refined into robust solutions.

2. **Agility and Customization:** Enterprises, especially those adopting SaaS solutions, frequently want deeper customization. Low-code tools let them adapt or integrate the SaaS platform to unique operational processes. This agility is particularly valuable in fast-evolving sectors or where compliance mandates frequent workflow alterations.

3. **Citizen Development:** Empowering non-developers can lighten the load on central IT teams. Business users can maintain or update forms, rules, or dashboards themselves, freeing developers to focus on higher-level architecture or advanced integrations.

Self-Service Integration

No-code platforms often incorporate **visual integration builders** for connecting SaaS systems with external APIs, data warehouses, or event streams. A marketing manager might, for example, integrate a CRM lead list with an email marketing tool, define triggers for campaigns, and track conversions in a single, self-service environment. This approach can accelerate innovation and reduce friction, provided appropriate governance is in place.

Industry-Specific Solutions

Certain industries—healthcare, finance, manufacturing—have historically lagged in adopting custom automation due to regulatory complexity or limited developer availability. Low-code/no-code SaaS offerings specialized in these domains enable subject matter experts (e.g., nurses, bankers, plant managers) to tailor solutions to specific regulations and operational flows without waiting for large IT backlogs.

10.3.2 Challenges and Limitations

While no-code/low-code solutions promise speed and democratization, they come with constraints that must be addressed carefully:

1. **Scalability and Performance:** Graphical rule engines or drag-and-drop workflows can generate suboptimal code or rely on interpretive runtimes. In high-scale scenarios, these auto-generated artifacts might become bottlenecks. Providers must offer advanced optimizations or fallback paths to custom code for heavy loads.

2. **Governance and Security:** Giving non-technical staff the ability to create and modify SaaS logic can introduce risk if not governed properly. Misconfigured integrations or data exposures are more likely when individuals without security training build flows that handle sensitive data. A robust governance framework—complete with role-based permissions, approvals, and versioning—is essential.

3. **Limited Flexibility:** No-code platforms typically rely on prebuilt templates or "building blocks." While these blocks can handle common tasks elegantly, custom or niche requirements might exceed the platform's available functionality. Organizations risk hitting a "ceiling" where advanced features or unique business logic require skilled developers to extend or bypass the no-code environment.

4. **Maintenance Over Time:** Citizen-developed applications might become critical to business operations but lack structured documentation or consistent design patterns. Without a clear maintenance plan or oversight, these solutions can accumulate technical debt. Over time, patchwork solutions across multiple departments can become a hidden burden that requires an IT-led consolidation effort.

Future Outlook

Low-code/no-code platforms will continue to evolve, integrating AI/ML-based "suggestions" that automatically propose workflows or data mappings. The synergy between AI, which can interpret user goals, and visual building interfaces can further reduce the complexity of creating new SaaS functionality. Additionally, expansions into **no-code integration** (similar to iPaaS—Integration Platform as a Service) can accelerate cross-system orchestration. The challenge for SaaS providers is to incorporate these capabilities in a way that maintains performance, reliability, and security, while also ensuring advanced users have an escape hatch for custom code.

10.4 Additional Emerging Trends in SaaS

While AI, edge computing, and no-code/low-code platforms arguably dominate current conversations about the future of SaaS, several **complementary developments** also deserve attention. Individually or in tandem, they may reshape how SaaS solutions are designed, delivered, and consumed over the next five to ten years.

10.4.1 Multi-Cloud and Cross-Cloud Orchestration

Motivation

Enterprises increasingly adopt multi-cloud or hybrid-cloud strategies to optimize costs, reduce vendor lock-in, or meet regional compliance mandates. As SaaS usage intensifies, providers may need to support multiple deployment targets seamlessly.

1. **Cross-Cloud Container Platforms:** Tools like Anthos (Google), Azure Arc (Microsoft), and open-source solutions can unify container orchestration across multiple clouds, letting SaaS developers deploy microservices to whichever region or provider best suits them. This approach extends multi-tenancy beyond a single cloud boundary.

2. **Data Fabric and Federation:** Multi-cloud data solutions allow queries spanning multiple databases or data lakes across different cloud providers. For SaaS that processes large data volumes or provides analytics features, such cross-cloud data integration can be a key differentiator.

3. **Challenges in Multi-Cloud:** Each cloud provider has unique abstractions, security models, and networking configurations. Achieving consistent performance, cost governance, and reliability is non-trivial. Observability also becomes more complex, requiring vendor-neutral solutions that unify logs, metrics, and traces across clouds.

10.4.2 Micro Frontends and Frontend Evolution

Beyond Microservices

Microservices revolutionized backend architectures, but large SaaS platforms can still suffer from monolithic frontends that are hard to maintain and scale. **Micro frontends** decompose the UI into modular, independently deployable components, each potentially owned by different teams. These components communicate with each other or orchestrate data retrieval through shared APIs.

1. **Dynamic Composition:** A micro frontend architecture might load the relevant UI modules on-the-fly, enabling each SaaS domain or feature to evolve independently. Updates to one

feature do not necessitate a full redeployment of the entire frontend codebase.

2. **Tech Stack Flexibility:** Different micro frontends can use distinct frameworks (React, Vue, Angular), letting teams pick the best tool for their domain or even progressively adopt new frameworks without rewriting the whole application.

3. **User Experience Coordination:** While micro frontends promise agility, they can introduce UI inconsistency if not carefully governed. Establishing common design systems, CSS guidelines, and cross-micro-frontend communication protocols ensures a coherent user experience.

10.4.3 Data Mesh and Distributed Data Governance

With the proliferation of data sources and specialized data processing pipelines, a new paradigm—**data mesh**—has emerged. In this model, data is organized by **domain** rather than centralized in large data lakes or warehouses. Each domain (e.g., finance, marketing, product analytics) owns its data as a "product" with well-defined interfaces, quality metrics, and discoverability. SaaS providers adopting data mesh approaches can deliver more flexible analytics and reporting tools:

1. **Domain-Centric Ownership:** Each domain is responsible for cleaning, transforming, and serving its data. SaaS solutions must provide robust metadata management, versioning, and user-friendly catalogs so that consumers from other domains can easily find and integrate the data.

2. **Self-Service Infrastructure:** The data mesh concept thrives on standardized tooling—such as data pipelines, governance frameworks, and policy engines—that domain teams can access without heavy overhead. SaaS architects must integrate these tools with existing multi-tenant data models.\

3. **Security and Interoperability:** Because data is spread across multiple domains, consistent security policies and identity management are crucial. A data mesh must also ensure that data transformations remain interoperable across different schemas and systems.

10.4.4 Advanced Developer Experience

The future of SaaS also hinges on improved developer experiences (DX). With the SaaS market saturated and smaller players vying for developer mindshare, offering seamless developer onboarding, comprehensive documentation, and user-friendly toolchains becomes vital.

1. **Frictionless Onboarding:** Clear, consistent APIs; well-documented SDKs in multiple languages; sample applications; and interactive tutorials can drastically reduce time-to-hello-world for new integrators. SaaS providers who excel at developer onboarding will naturally attract more usage and loyalty.

2. **Infrastructure as Code (IaC) Extensions:** As more enterprises automate their SaaS resource provisioning (for example, setting up tenant configurations or user roles), providers that offer Terraform modules or other IaC integrations stand out. This approach allows DevOps teams to treat SaaS resources like any other piece of infrastructure.

3. **Continuous Collaboration:** Modern developer portals might incorporate real-time feedback loops, chat-based support with developers from the SaaS vendor, or advanced sandboxes that replicate production environments for safe experimentation. The synergy of developer communities fosters ecosystem growth and robust third-party extensions.

10.4.5 Quantum Computing and Specialized Hardware

While still largely experimental in mainstream contexts, **quantum computing** and specialized hardware accelerators (e.g., TPUs, FPGAs) could eventually impact how SaaS platforms handle computationally intensive tasks:

1. **Potential Use Cases:** Complex optimization problems, cryptography, large-scale machine learning, or advanced simulations could benefit from quantum acceleration. Early adopters in finance or pharmaceuticals might see a competitive edge with quantum-enabled SaaS modules.

2. **Integration Challenges:** Quantum hardware remains scarce and specialized. A future "quantum-enabled SaaS architecture" might offer HPC (High-Performance Computing) or quantum backend services on demand, bridging classical cloud infrastructures with quantum co-processors.

3. **Timeline and Pragmatic Outlook:** Although quantum computing hype is high, widespread SaaS usage is likely a decade away for most applications. Nonetheless, forward-thinking SaaS providers keep an eye on specialized hardware breakthroughs, ensuring they remain prepared if quantum or advanced HPC technologies become more commercially viable.